Walking the Road to God

WHY I LEFT EVERYTHING BEHIND AND TOOK TO THE STREETS TO SAVE SOULS

Father Lawrence Carney

Caritas Press, Arizona, USA

WALKING THE ROAD TO GOD

Published with ecclesiastical approval

Father Lawrence Carney

First Edition

10 9 8 7 6 5 4 3 2 1

ISBN: 978-1-940209-33-3

To Our Lady of Perpetual Help, who inspired me to become a priest and helped me to stop running from my vocation.

And to Our Lady of Sorrows, who seems to answer every prayer and allows me to mingle my tears with hers at the foot of the cross on behalf of her wandering souls.

CARITAS PRESS

CaritasPress.org

AUTHOR'S INTRODUCTION

As a seminarian at Mount Saint Mary's in Emmitsburg, Maryland, I often wondered and even asked my teachers, "How are we going to bring souls into the Catholic Church?" As a parish priest, and later as a chaplain for nuns, I decided to pray the Rosary while walking in town. People always come to talk to me while I'm on my walks. Following is how this book, through providence, came to be.

After walking around St. Joseph, Missouri, for about a year, the local newspaper contacted me and wanted to interview me about why I am a walking priest. The interview was done well and it got attention on the internet. In regard to my writing, I put the project in Our Lady's hands and asked for guidance from Providence. About six months later, a publisher contacted me after seeing the newspaper article, and asked if I ever considered writing a book. This was an answer to prayer. And so this book is in your hands. This is God's book, not mine.

I want to first thank God for the opportunity to serve Him as a missionary in search of souls. I also thank my parents, The Martinian Prayer Warriors, The Benedictines of Mary Queen of Apostles as well as members of other convents and monasteries and all others who have offered prayers on behalf of my ministry.

CONTENTS

"But as the Lord hath distributed to every one, as God hath called every one: so let him walk.

1 Corinthians 7:17

1

They Call Me the "Walking Priest"

Standing on the corner, waiting for the light to turn green on a cool spring afternoon in St. Joseph, Missouri, I had no way of knowing that God was about to give me the happiest year of my life. I had just finished praying a Rosary as I walked the city streets, something I did quite often – at least five or six times a week. I wrapped the beads around my wrist, set my backpack down and reached inside for my book. A prayer card of St. Francis de Sales marked the section, "The Formation of the Apostles of the Latter Times." The light turned green. As I crossed the street, I read this passage from *True Devotion To Mary*: "They shall carry...the Crucifix in their right hand and the Rosary in their left hand..."[1]

I thought, "I need to do that!"

Tucked in my sash, I just so happened to have a beautiful twelve-inch Crucifix that I had received in a mysterious way. A few weeks before, my mother had delivered some things I left back in Wichita. This very old Crucifix, made of dark

---

[1]   *True Devotion to Mary*, St. Louis de Montfort, Tan, 1985, no. 59, p. 35.

wood, with a metal corpus, showed up. It had come to me only a few weeks after I had started walking around town, praying the Rosary. I knew I needed to do something with this special Crucifix, so I put it between my cassock and sash, thinking it would make too much of a spectacle to carry it in my hand. But after reading those words: "They shall carry... the Crucifix in their right hand the Rosary in their left hand..." I was convicted. I thought, "Well, what do I have to lose? St. Louis de Montfort predicted someone would do this, so why not me?"

I took the Rosary off my wrist and pulled the Crucifix out of my sash like a sword. As I began to pray the Rosary, people started honking. I usually waved, but now, I chuckled a bit to myself as I returned their greeting by raising the Crucifix in the air.

Christ the King has come to claim the city of St. Joseph," I thought, "and I am His ambassador!"

Serving Jesus in the streets of the city is my joy. It brings me great happiness to meet people who come up to me with a question about God or a comment about how they always see me walking and think about God. Some honk their horns, some give me a thumbs up. My purpose is to direct people with good hearts to the heart of God.

"My sheep have wandered in every mountain, and in every high hill: and my flocks were scattered upon the face of the earth, and there was none that sought them, there was none, I say, that sought them." [2]

I began my Rosary walks a number of years ago when I was a parish priest. It was not difficult to see the fruits. One day, while I was still a parish pastor, I was walking and praying a Rosary in the city when a man in his mid-sixties pulled up beside me in his muddy, old truck and called out: "Father, do you do drive-through Confessions?"

"Come on over," I said, putting my beads in my pocket.

Traffic was beginning to stack up behind his car, so he

---

[2]   Ezekiel xxxiv: 6.

drove a little way and parked in a lot. I stood beside his truck as we had a friendly chat through his window. Then he asked. "Father can I go to confession?"

I pulled out my stole and climbed into his truck. Then he gave me a lift to the parish, where he made his confession in the confessional. I absolved him. His face changed from a kind of cloudy appearance to one of clarity. After a number of years, he became a leader in the parish. The sacrament changed him forever. But I have to wonder where he would be today if he hadn't seen a priest walking down the street.

Another time, a lady in her mid-eighties called the parish to begin classes to become Catholic. After about a year, she said that she was not ready. Her parents raised her to be a good Protestant. She lamented the idea of "turning her back on them" to become Catholic. I walked over to her house a few times to visit, in hopes that she would continue with her initial desire to convert. After those visits proved futile, I entrusted her into the Blessed Virgin Mary's hands. Since I had been doing the Rosary walks for a few years at the time, I had developed a routine and followed the same route each day. But one day, when I came to this woman's house, I did something different. I paused and thought about paying her a visit. But then I was inspired to keep walking and storm heaven for her conversion. The next day she called me and said, "Father, I saw the Blessed Virgin Mary appear at the foot of my bed. Then I saw you walk by my window praying the Rosary. I want to complete my entry into the Catholic Church."

With joy, I exclaimed, "Welcome home!"

That was back in the day when I was a pastor in a couple of small Kansas towns. But I had developed this burning desire to be in a community of religious, so I asked my bishop if I could go, and he gave me permission. I was granted a sabbatical to discern my vocation within the priesthood. So I booked air passage to Europe for over three months to visit a few communities that I might possibly join. I started

9

my journey in Rome, attending a conference on the Sacred Liturgy. One day, while I was walking around Rome, an Italian lady stopped me and asked me a question: "If I buy you a saturno, will you wear it?"

I said, "Yes."

A saturno, named after the planet, is a black formal clerical hat with a rounded top, black bow and a large convex rim. The lady paid the vendor next to St. Peter's Square and the hat was mine. When I first saw it, I thought of the priests in the movies. My next thought was: "This is going to be practical."

In a few weeks, I was going to walk the ancient pilgrimage: *El Camino de Compostela* in Spain. Since the walk was scheduled for thirty-two days in the middle of the grueling Spanish summer, the sun was going to be relentless. So the hat would be fitting in many ways. It would help me keep from getting over-heated and sunburned. It was also a fitting hat to wear with the cassock. I had worn a cassock every day for four years. But little did I know that the saturno would be a magnet for the curious. It made a statement. "Here is someone set apart for God. Come see what a life lived for the love of Jesus is like."

The first time I wore it, I felt a little awkward, to say the least. A very serious-looking priest walked by in his clericals – a black shirt and pants. He looked at me for a moment and then just kept walking, shaking his head in disgust. I thought, "Well, what is the big deal? I have to keep my promise to the Italian lady."

"Each person was born to pray and be in union with God, and priests were ordained to encourage souls to come closer to Jesus. After I was ordained to the Priesthood, I personally observed, in the life of a parish priest, how powerful the connection is between the soul of the priest and the souls of the sheep when they are hungry for God, and the priest is ordained to feed the world with God's love."

"I admit that it is burdensome to direct individual souls, but it is a burden that gives great comfort, just like that of the reapers and the grape harvesters, who are never more content than when they have lots of work and when they return from the fields fully laden. It is a work which refreshes the heart because of the happiness that those who undertake it experience.

St. Francis de Sales

2

Under Mary's Mantle

I walk past miles of retail shops on a busy road. Well, maybe not busy for New York City. But busy for a small city like St. Joseph. It is one of those clear, hot days. There are many of those days in this city, and I walk through them all, dressed in long-sleeved black from head to toe, with a single purpose.

A man in his late thirties drives into a parking lot just ahead. He's in a white Lincoln. He rolls down his window. Something about me puzzles him.

"What are you doing?" he asks with a hint of sarcasm.

I stop praying and smile at him.

"I'm fishing."

He laughs. "What do you mean?"

"See," I say. "This Crucifix is the hook, and the beads are the line. If you get out of the car, I can show you what I mean."

He turns off his engine and gets out.

"May I?" I ask if I can put the Rosary around his neck. I got this idea from St. Louis de Montfort's biography. Everyone who touched his Rosary converted or reverted to the Catholic faith.

The man gives me permission, so I put the Rosary around his neck and tug it lightly.

"See? You have just been caught!" I say. He laughs again, hysterically.

We spend the next hour talking. He tells me he was pagan until twenty-three, when he began to read his way into the Lutheran Church. He tells me how impressed he was by my walking and praying. He asks about the Cassock. I tell him it was blessed in the old Roman Ritual as a sacramental, which is an object instituted by the Church to give grace. It has the form of a robe to imitate our Savior who wore a robe. It is black to signify our mourning for Jesus, whom they crucified.

We discuss the Bible and morals. He speaks from his Lutheran perspective, and I speak from Catholic truths. As the sun sets, he says he has to go because he has an hour drive in front of him.

"Can I just tell you one more thing?" I ask. I tell him about the four transcendentals: goodness, beauty, truth and oneness. These are four qualities of God, and people are drawn to Him by these four ways. Experts claim that ninety percent learn about God primarily through beauty. I explain to Michael that, based on our conversation, I can tell truth is the door by which he enters. He read himself into Christianity, and I can tell he comes to understand things through reason. We exchange contact information, and he leaves.

Being a spiritual father on the streets means being available for those whom God puts in my path. When a child needs something, he comes to his father and asks. I wait and see which spiritual children will come to me. Sometimes, they look at me and hesitate, but then they come up and ask their question. Children have to let their father know that they are hungry. When they approach me, the first thing I do is smile. Then, I listen and respond to their questions or whatever they want to share. If there's a pause, I keep the conversation going by asking, "What is your story?" A father listens and is interested in his child. When people tell me their stories, they are speaking from their hearts. Then, I can speak from my heart, a heart that has been contemplating God as I walk. I feed these children who come to me with my meditations on the mystery of God and often they do receive the spiritual nourishment I offer them. That is great joy!

A few months after I "caught" Michael with my Rosary "fishing net," he calls and invites me over. A great peace permeates his home. His wife and children are so happy I am here. They prepared spaghetti especially for me because I am part Italian.

"I have told my Lutheran friends about you. They want to meet this priest who walks around St. Joseph."

I am all for it.

Michael tells me he thinks he is a descendent of St. Margaret of Scotland.

Now I am sure. "This family will come to the Catholic Church some day!" I say to myself.

Some days later, we meet at Dunkin Donuts. We talk about apostolic succession and morality.

"It has been an hour so we probably should wrap it up," I tell him.

"Really? I am having fun. I do not want to go yet."

So our debate continues for two more hours.

I am well aware that I will need a long-term outlook for the work I do. I am OK with that. I try to follow in the footsteps of great saints. After three years, St. Francis de Sales, one of history's greatest preachers, had no converts. But he had 72,000 after twenty-five years. The Church was stronger then than it is now. It seems the devil has been unleashed in these times, and he is very powerful. Nonetheless, there will be conversions if I am given the grace to persevere. Real conversion usually takes a long time.

And imagine if there were more than just one walking priest. Imagine fifty men in habits walking around little St. Joseph. This is my dream and the reason I envision a new order of priests, clerics and brothers.

As it is now, I have powerful allies. The sisters for whom I am a chaplain have their work cut out for them. I used to write down all the names of the people I would meet on my walks and then ask the Benedictines of Mary, Queen of Apostles to pray for them individually. But that took so much time that now I just tell them new stories of the people I meet and ask them to pray for anyone I am going to meet. From time to time, I beg them to remember how it is a privilege to pray for souls on the streets. I encourage them as they grow from glory to glory in their spiritual life, becoming ever more perfect, that they are saving thousands of souls individually. My encounters with people on the streets give the sisters context that spurs them on ever more in this endeavor.

As for my part, I need to become as reverent as St. Gregory the Great or St. Padre Pio because mystics say that, if a priest would celebrate Mass with the reverence of these priests, it would be easier for the world to convert.

The streets of St. Joseph are full of reminders. I remember many different souls individually, especially when I go back to certain places where I met them. I speak to heaven that the grace of God help them come closer to Him.

I cross an intersection and notice a man sitting in his parked car. I greet him with a smile, gently raise my Crucifix and keep walking. You might be thinking, "Why didn't you go and talk to him?"

Imagine a man walking down a sidewalk in a cassock, and some people sitting on a porch. I would estimate that the majority of people sitting on that porch see this man and immediately think, "Who is that? I do not want him to come interrupt our peace." So I make it a rule to smile, wave the Crucifix and walk by. Some people probably think, "Why didn't he stop and talk to us? Now I am curious." So they speak up and ask me to come and chat. The man in the car doesn't ask. Not today. He will on another day, after we greet each other with a smile and my raised Crucifix two more times – the first about a month later and the next two weeks after that, at the exact same intersection.

"Father, I have seen you three times," he tells me. "Each time I see you I am having a bad day. But after I see you, my day is blessed."

We talk for a few minutes. I find out that he waits there to pick up his friend from work. He tells me that he left the Catholic Church three years ago and tried to kill himself.

"God does not want you to live this way," I tell him. "He wants you to be happy in this life and in the next." I give him a bulletin from a nearby church where I am staying and encourage him to come to Confession and just come to talk. He says he will.

He makes good on that promise and comes to me in tears one day after the sung Latin Mass. He asks me how to become a member of the parish. He then attends regularly until moving out of town.

My walk is also fruitful with the very young. Some of the kids in the neighborhood see me walking and run over to satisfy their curiosity. Many of them ask, "Could we have a 'necklace?'"

I tell them, "Children, these are not necklaces, but Rosaries. The Blessed Virgin Mary appeared to St. Dominic in 1214 in a vision and gave him the Rosary. See those roses over there? Many Christians would take rose petals, dry them, crush them, make a ball, put a hole in them, and put a string in them. These people would say the words the illustrious Archangel Gabriel spoke to Mary, 'Hail, full of grace...' over and over to keep in mind how God had mercy on us."

The children listen intently. I ask them if they would like to play Catholic Trivia. "How many persons are there in the Trinity? Can you name three of the Apostles? What is the name of the Mother of God?" I line them up, according to who was first to raise his hand and get the right answer. Then they get to pick which color Rosary they want. We play these games from time to time, and I have new prizes—medals that people no longer want and have given to me. The children pick out a medal and I explain each one.

"Oh, you picked the miraculous medal. See that prayer, 'O Mary, conceived without sin, pray for us who have recourse to thee.' You should put this around your neck and pray that prayer often."

"Oh, you picked a medal of St. Joseph. He was the foster father of Jesus, you know the one on this Crucifix." I show them the nails and Jesus' wounds.

Sometimes the children run up to me and want to get Rosaries for their friends.

Once, a kind lady named Joan brought five hundred Rosaries for me to bless. We put them out on the wall next to the sidewalk. As I was getting out my stole, the Epiphany Water and the Roman Ritual to bestow the blessing, three children came up on their bikes asking for Rosaries again.

I say, "You can only have some Rosaries if you gather about a dozen kids right now."

As I am waiting, I bless other items—medals and Crucifixes—that Joan donated. When all the kids show up, I tell them, "OK, fold your hands very carefully and place them across your breast. Now lift your heart up to God. I am going to bless these Rosaries in Latin. Ask God to bless you as I say the blessing for these Rosaries. Remember to take an extra Rosary to give to a friend." I say the prayers in Latin. The kids are all very quiet. After the blessing, I hand out Rosaries. The kids are putting two around their necks. One said, "I am bringing one of these to school for my friend."

"That is wonderful!" I reply. "Mary is getting into the public school where I am forbidden to enter."

I walk by the house of one of the mothers of these children. Her friend is talking to her on the porch and asks me to come over. They are consoling each other because of some problems they are having. The mother asks, "Are you the Father who gives out Rosaries to my daughter?"

The girl, about eight years old, often comes to speak to me while I am walking through the neighborhood.

"Father, although my daughter is ordinarily reserved and doesn't talk much, she loves to talk to you. She comes home to tell me that you smiled and said, 'hello.' Come inside and see the shrine she has made. It contains all the Rosaries and prayer cards that you have given her."

So I go inside and find myself fighting back tears.

Handing out Rosaries is such an easy way to preach the Kingdom of God. The children come up and learn how to pray. They learn the faith.

"Father, could you give me a Rosary too," the girl's mother asks, "and teach me how to pray it?" We talk about her family and God for about half an hour. As I am leaving the girl comes up on her bike, and I just smile upon seeing her radiant face, saying "Hello."

"Mary, please take her under your mantel and make her become a saint!" I pray silently.

"atience is power.

Venerable Archbishop
Fulton J. Sheen

3

Sharing My Happiness

When I first came to St. Joseph, I was happy to see that St. Patrick's Church was situated in the center of the city. I find that the heart of a large city is ideal for the Rosary walks, first because, strategically, it is best to be in the center so I can carry the gospel message out to all the edges of the city, like a hub and spokes. Second, our cities are in dire need of spiritual renewal.

The square in the center of St. Joseph is quaint and pretty. They have new, black iron benches throughout the area, and I like to sit there. The square hosts many outdoor events -- jazz festivals, battle of the bands, car shows, a Pumpkin Festival, motorcycle shows, among other things. I like to take my tea break on these benches and pray the Divine Office, an arrangement of psalms, texts from scripture and the saints and liturgical readings to be prayed throughout the day. It is also known as the Liturgy of the Hours. I find that when I sit and pray, people usually come up to talk. The Psalms of None, which are prayed at 3 p.m., speak of the difficult hours of the soul and the judgment of the King of the Cross, Our Lord Jesus

Christ. Many of the people who walk by have worked for most of the day and are taking their break or leaving work. I find this an excellent time to meet people. The Psalms correspond with the general sentiments of the people whom I meet; namely, they are hungry for God and are enduring the difficulties of a Godless culture.

The owner of a tattoo parlor comes up to speak with me.

"What are you doing?" he asks.

I pick up the Crucifix which is lying on the bench and explain my fishing technique.

He looks at my Roman Breviary and says, "What is that black book?"

"I pray the Psalms eight times a day, I explain. "This allows me to pray all one hundred-fifty Psalms each week. Right now I am praying that men of goodwill come up to talk to me."

He laughs and says that he needs to go.

The owner of the Martini bar comes up to me and starts a similar conversation. In the middle of the conversation he asks, "What is your story?"

I tell him how God put me here in St. Joseph, Missouri.

"So here I am," I say.

He laughs. "Well it's getting close to four, I need to open the bar."

About a month later I sit on the bench to continue my Rosary. Both the tattoo parlor owner and the martini bar owner approach me and say, "What is going on?"

"I am just praying for your conversion."

They both laugh.

"What do you have there?" one of them asks me.

I explain the Rosary to them.

The tattoo parlor owner says, "May I have one?"

The martini bar owner echoes, "Yes, can I have one, too?"

"What is your favorite color?"

After they each pick a Rosary from my bag, I hand each of them the pamphlet, "How to Pray the Rosary."

I point out the beads to the diagram the Nuns had produced on the little pamphlet. Then I ask, "Would you like to practice one of the prayers?"

They both agree, so a martini bar owner and a tattoo parlor owner are praying a Rosary together with me in the square of St. Joseph while a number of passers-by look on. I wish I knew what they were thinking.

"Repeat after me," I say, "Hail Mary..."

Since then, these two men kindly greet me when I run into them from time to time around town. One day, they both approach me as usual.

"How are you, Padre?"

"I am better than ever. Would you like to pick out a sacred medal?"

They look at me with questions on their faces. I pull out my plastic bag of sacred medals, grab about fifty, put the bag down and present the pile to them with both hands. They each smile and in turn search through the pile, picking one out and asking about it, putting it back down and fingering through until they each find one they like. I explain very briefly about each of them, "Oh, St. Benedict's medal. That one has an exorcism and a blessing. There is lot to say about it, but let me point out a few letters on the back. V. R. S. *Vade retro satana,* 'Get behind me Satan!' These are the words of Jesus in response to Peter's concern about the impending Crucifixion of Jesus. I tell the new owner of the St. Benedict's medal, When our souls are in danger from the devil, we do well to say the words of Jesus, 'Get behind me Satan!'"

He says, "Wow, that is cool!"

The other one picks out a Miraculous Medal. "Padre, can you tell me about this one?"

"Yes, when I was in Paris, France, a couple of years ago, I went to see the incorrupt body of St. Catherine Laboure.

It is on *Rue due Bac* where anyone may enter to see the place where the Blessed Virgin Mary appeared and asked St. Catherine to have these medals cast. Look at both of her hands. Do you see the rays coming out? During her vision, St. Catherine wondered why some rays are bright, but others seem to be missing. The Blessed Virgin Mary explained that graces are dispensed through her hands when people ask for them. However, people often neglect to ask for the graces she would like to give us, so that is why no light comes from her hands in some parts of the image."

"That is interesting," he says. "I am going to have to wear this medal. We need to get back to work."

"Before you go," I say, "I want to point out the prayer on your medal. 'O Mary conceived without sin, pray for us who have recourse to thee.' If you pray the prayer often, the Blessed Virgin Mary will intercede for you to receive the graces of God to be good. Gentlemen, since you must go, may I give you my priestly blessing?"

I give the blessing, and they depart, medals in hand and something new to ponder in their hearts.

On Friday afternoon, before the Battle of the Bands in the square, I sit on that familiar bench. I have the Crucifix on the bench beside me, along with a bag of Rosaries and sacred medals. I am praying None. A woman and two men in their late twenties come up and say, "What is going on here?"

I close my breviary, smile and say, "I am praying the Psalms."

"Are you giving things away?"

"Yes do you see anything you like?"

"What is in the bag?" they ask eagerly.

"Oh, those are sacred medals. Would you each like to pick one?"

I scoop up a pile of medals in both my hands and extend them toward the three. After they each pick one, I explain briefly what they chose.

"St. Peregrine is the patron saint of cancer. He did a lot of penance and developed a blood disease on his leg. But after fervent prayers and penance, he was miraculously cured. Many people receive favors from his intercession."

"Oh, that is St. Joseph. He is the foster father of Jesus. This town is named St. Joseph, so you got a good one."

The last one held up her new treasure, "Oh, that is Our Lady of Perpetual Help! There is a special painting in Rome close to St. Mary Major on the Esquiline Hill. The child Jesus was running from two angels who were carrying the implements of his future Crucifixion. You cannot see it in the medal, but His sandal is dangling to show how He ran with haste into the arms of His mother. I have a personal story about this sacred image. When I was six years old, I was in kindergarten at a parochial school. Fr. Miller gave each of the children a holy card of Our Lady of Perpetual Help. He said, 'Children, hold the card and extend your arm in front of your face. Now move the card back and forth while looking at Mary's eyes. Notice how she is looking at you. She is always there to protect you.' After he said those words, I saw real eyes looking at me. I thought to myself, 'If a priest can make that happen, I want to be a priest!' I will never forget that priest. He wore a black habit with a big Rosary on the side. That is about the only thing I remembered in Kindergarten, except when we slept on the floor with our mats, graham crackers and milk. About twenty years later, I went into that Kindergarten room with my mother. As I entered, I noticed a tabernacle there with the Most Holy Sacrament of the Altar. I knelt down immediately in awe. I remembered when Fr. Miller told us of Our Lady of Perpetual Help, he was standing in the front of the room, where now the tabernacle stood. Jesus was now there in his place, under the appearance of bread. I saw the powerful connection between the priesthood and Jesus, and I took that as a sign from God that I must stop running away from the priesthood. So at the age of twenty-five I entered the Seminary."

After these stories, I speak a little about my current assignment with the Benedictines of Mary Queen of the Apostles. I speak about the Latin Mass and Gregorian Chant. One of the three speaks up.

"Father, we are part of a band. But I grew up in Colorado and I used to be part of a Latin Choir in the Catholic Church. I love Latin!"

We talk for awhile and he tells me he no longer attends the Catholic Church. I encourage him and his friends, "The sacred language of Latin is so beautiful. Look at these CD's. The Benedictines of Mary, Queen of the Apostles make music so they can build their monastery. They have hit the top of Billboard's Classical Traditional Music Chart the last three years in a row!"

After a cordial conversation, they explain they need to get ready for the evening's concert. I give them my blessing and continue with my prayers. I don't know what will result from our providential conversation, but maybe a seed has been planted.

✝ (IHS) ✝ (IHS) ✝ (IHS) ✝ (IHS) ✝

I am walking close to the square in St. Joseph when I see three men in their fifties. The one with a very large beard stares at me for a while—a long while—and then continues on his way. I forget about it very quickly. Months later, I am walking in the poor part of town. As I am praying a decade of the Rosary for conversion, that same man, standing in front of his very old dilapidated house, yells something at me to get my attention. I turn and hear him speaking in broken English, with an Eastern European accent. Once I get to him, he takes my hand and kisses the back of it. Some may not know it but the hands of a priest are consecrated, they are sacramentals, they hold the Body and Blood of Jesus Christ on the altar. At one time it was a custom to greet a priest by either kissing the back of his hand or touching the back of his hand to the forehead.

He then looks at me and says, "Are you a priest?"

"Oh yes I am a priest."

"May I kiss?" He points at the Crucifix.

"Yes."

He kisses the corpus very devoutly.

He continues in broken English, "I used to be priest."

I am shocked and ask, "Really? What kind of a priest?"

He responds, "I used to be Eastern Orthodox. I used to have..." His hands make the motion of one putting on a sports jacket and he points at my black garment.

"Cassock?"

"Yes, I used to wear."

"Do you still have it?"

"Yes. You see! You see!"

He invites me into his home and goes into his closet, and takes some things off a high shelf. He pulls out an old cassock and shows it to me.

"Put it on!" I say.

He smiles and excitedly puts on the cassock. Then he pulls out a chasuble, the outer garment the priest wears for the Holy Sacrifice of the Mass. His was an Eastern Orthodox chasuble. A single stole on the outside of the chasuble hangs from the neck on the front and back. It signifies the authority of Jesus, while the chasuble signifies the charity of Jesus. After he puts it on, he has a very big smile and a glimmer in his eyes.

He then shows me a very old red book. I don't know what language, maybe it is Greek. It is a Missal, a book used for the Mass.

"Book over one hundred years old," he says "Very old."

After he shows me his sacred things, we go back outside. He explains to me why he no longer practices his priesthood. He tells me his problems. He looks at me and begins to cry.

"You nice priest," he says.

He repeats this a number of times, kisses the Crucifix and my hands many times. After he tells me his sins, I say, "God wants you to be happy."

I encourage him to leave his sinful life behind. "Come to church and go to Confession." He nods his head in agreement.

I have not seen him since that day, but I keep praying for him and blessing his house when I walk by.

I keep imagining, "What if he came back into full practice of his priesthood?"

Saints and doctors of the church say we do not comprehend the power of the priesthood. A priest is encouraged to say Mass every day. Every Mass extends the Kingdom of God. We will not know the value of one Mass until entering eternity. I continue to think, "I hope we can get that priest to say the Holy Sacrifice of the Mass again. Calvary is represented every time a priest says Mass. That would really help to bring about a swifter conversion of the people in St. Joseph, Missouri."

I am waiting on the sidewalk when a young man gets out of a truck and says, "Hey can I walk with you?"

"Yes, would you like to get some coffee?" I pointed at the Hardees down the block.

"Yes. I have seen you around town a lot. I thought to myself, if I see you again I am just going to get out and ask if I can walk with you."

James is a country boy who loves Jesus. He is just a simple, happy young man. During our coffee, he tells me his life story and a very heroic deed he did. He tells me his sinful life and his path to Jesus.

After drinking our coffee, I challenge him, "James, it seems like God has entered your life. There are many stories of saints who have lived very sinful lives and have come to

Jesus. We read about people like St. Augustine. I think God has big plans for you since you have lived in sin and have seen a great light.

James contacts me a few times and we get together. He has me over for a meal. He shows me his Christian music. Another time, he invites me to a Chinese Restaurant. He tells me about his problems at work. After he lands another job, he begins working so much that we no longer get together. I continue to have the nuns pray for him and I pray myself for his continued conversion to the Catholic Faith. God will provide. It takes time for God to work on a soul. I am not sure what God has in mind, but I think it would be helpful to have more city-monks to aid in the work for the conversion of all souls. I think a community of evangelists walking the streets would reproduce the image of Jesus walking around with his apostles and disciples. As far as James goes, if he sees me again, I think he would like to follow-up about how his life is going. If we had more walking around town in the holy Cassock, it would increase the chances of him being reminded of the treasures of the Catholic Church. This is my dream, a new religious community called the Canons Regular of St. Martin of Tours.

One day, I am walking from North Kansas City to Downtown Kansas City, across the river. I celebrate Mass at Old St. Patrick's. I've been in the habit of walking four miles to the evening Mass. There is a little section close to the river called "Little Italy." As I approach this part of town, a van pulls up. The driver rolls down her window. "We saw you crossing the bridge," she says. "Do you need a ride?"

"Thanks for the offer," I reply. "I am only a few blocks from Holy Rosary Parish. I want to stop in to pray before I go to say Mass at Old St. Patrick's."

"Aren't you a little hot in that black..."

I fill in the blank, "...Cassock."

I continue, "It is just a little hot, but I unite my sacrifice with Jesus." I show them the Crucifix. "I am a little sad. When I walked across the bridge the Crucifix of my Rosary fell off. Do you know any jewelry stores that could fix it?"

The driver surprisingly answers, "Father we are not Catholic, but I make Rosaries!"

"Well, that sounds like Divine Providence. Could you fix my Rosary?" I hand her the Rosary and she looks at it and says, "Yes."

We exchange contact information, and they drive off.

I continue my walk to "Little Italy." Unfortunately the church is locked, so I sit in a little memorial park called "Christopher Columbus." The jeweler calls me and tells me she has the Rosary tools. I tell her where I am, and she meets me there. She tells me the story of her Italian ancestors who settled in "Little Italy." After working on the Rosary, she and I say good-bye. This is one of many unfinished stories because we have not yet seen all that God has in store. St. Frances de Sales was instrumental in the conversion of 72,000 people. But something that people easily forget, according to his biographers, was that there were zero conversions or reversions in the first years! I am confident about taking the patient approach that he took. There will be a large catch because God will make it happen. This requires time, lots of time.

One day, a Protestant Pastor I met previously on one of my walks invites me to a Christian music festival held every Tuesday night. It was started by some of the local pastors.

When I get there, a number of people walk up and

welcome me. Some of them I had met on the Rosary walks, some had read the article about me in the local newspaper and some had seen me walking, but never had the chance to meet me. The conversations are exiting as I meet new people and exchange stories of people whom I had already met.

The Pastor of the place comes up to me and says, "Father we are so happy you have come to join us." He explains how his church helps people overcome their addictions.

"One of the ladies had struggled with problems. She went back and forth from addiction to responsibility. Then, she started making rugs in a cottage industry. She uses her creativity and has made hundreds of rugs. We go to the Farmer's Market in Kansas City to sell them. Customers love them because they know where they come from."

"Do you have a 'Made in U.S.A. tag?'"

He smiles and continues, "You will have to come in and see the little cottage industry we have here."

"Yes, I want to see it."

He shows me the looms first.

"Father, people donate their old clothes and we cut the fabric into strips."

He puts his hand in a bin and pulls out a wad of cloth. "Our slogan is, 'From drugs to rugs.' Our people go from the shreds of addiction to an ordered life, like the order of these rugs. People are separated in our society and taught that they are worthless. The system will put them on welfare. They lose a sense of dignity. We want these people to be creative, make something, and become financially established. These people can make a living making these rugs. People want to buy them."

After he shows me around, I go back outside to the music festival. One of the people brings over a hotdog, which I eat with relish. The pastor comes back, saying, "Father it was so good of you to look at our cottage industry. I hope you can come back."

"I really think you are on to something here," I say. "I, too, am an entrepreneur." I point up the hill at the Church of the Immaculate Conception. "You see that beautiful Gothic Revival Church? Isn't it beautiful?"

"Father, I used to attend that church!" he says.

We continue exchanging our dreams for a better world. I am so pleased I got to meet him. He explains he has to go attend to some things.

As I eat my hotdog, a man named Robert comes up to me. I first met him behind the counter at a gas station that is notorious for crime. I had gone in for a tea break and noticed a Rosary hanging from his neck and said, "I like your Rosary. If you ever need it blessed, I have the technology; namely, a stole, Epiphany water and the Roman Ritual." He smiled and agreed. I went to get my hot water, brewed my tea and poured in some ice. Upon leaving, I told him, "Whenever you are free, I will be outside." I went outside and leaned on the propane tank cage. A mother and her two boys and their friend had joined me, and I was sharing with them some stories about the Rosary walks. Robert came out for a break. "Father can you bless this now? I need to go inside." As he went back to his job at the counter, I took out my stole, Epiphany water and the Ritual. I blessed his Rosary in the Latin prayers. He came back out and was very thankful for the blessing. We departed.

A few months later I walked alone to the gas station, for a tea break. I greeted Robert and went to drink my tea on the propane tank cage. Robert came out saying, "Father, I lost that Rosary you blessed, can you bless another one for me?"

"Certainly. What color do you like?"

He picked out a color, and had to leave as a customer needed gas. He came back out and said, "Father can I give you a gift?" He handed me $20.

"Robert, you need that money for yourself," I said.

"No, Father God needs it."

"Yes, I will use it to feed the poor."

When I see him again at the Christian Music Festival, he tells me his eight-year old daughter wants to meet me.

I ask her, "My child, do you want to hold this Crucifix?" She shakes her head.

"Do you want a picture of the Mother of God and Jesus?" Again, she shakes her head.

She looked at my wrist where I had wrapped my Rosary. "Do you want to see this Rosary?" She nods.

I take it off my wrist and give it to her.

After a while, I tell her I need that Rosary back. "But would you like to pick one for yourself?"

(The Rosary was one that I had made. I used jade stones and a very strong sterling silver wire wrap. This virtually unbreakable model is one of the few that can withstand the rigors of the Rosary Walks. Sometimes I lose them, but a non-Catholic jewelry maker, whom I met on one of my walks, knows how to reproduce them.)

The little girl is happy to pick her own out from among the colorful plastic Rosaries I take from my bag.

"These Rosaries are sacred objects. They have been blessed by a priest. They are set apart for God alone. If anything happens to damage the Rosary, either bury it in the ground or give it to a Father like me. Never put the Rosary in the trash." I give her a pamphlet: *How to Pray the Rosary.* "Would you like to practice the words the Archangel Gabriel said to Mary, the Mother of Jesus?"

She nods. I kneel down to pray. Smiling at her, I say, "Repeat after me. Hail Mary..." She responds in a very soft voice, "Hail Mary..."

After we unite our hearts to God and the Mother of God, I open my eyes and notice that almost all the kids – about ten or so – have come up to watch us. When I stand up, they all want Rosaries. So I explain the Rosary briefly and give them pamphlets.

After they leave, Robert's mother comes up to me to

thank me. She offers me a gift of $20.

"How can any of you give me money when I know you have so little? I cannot take it from you."

She looks me in the eye and says, "Father, I will be offended greatly if you do not take it."

"I will buy some food for someone who is hungry."

That day comes soon enough. I walk by the Salvation Army, and a young man asks if he can have some money.

"Money I do not give out," I say, "but I will buy you food."

"I am hungry."

"There is a convenience store over there."

He agrees and we walk together. After he gives me his name, I ask him, "You were abused as a child, weren't you?"

"Yes, how did you know."

"Call it intuition."

After he picked out a burrito, chips and a drink, I pay for them, shake his hand and say, "God Bless."

As I walk away, I have an overpowering sense of my own unworthiness. I begin to pray, heart to heart, "God why did you choose me to be born to such a good family with loving parents? Why was he put in a family that abused him? I do not deserve my state in life. I thank you from the depths of my heart." I make a resolution to keep going forward with the Rosary walks. The passage from Scripture comes to mind, "And to whomever[2] much is given, of him much shall be required."

I once received a request to bless a house, where the owner had witnessed strange phenomena, such as shadows moving about, pictures flying off the wall and ugly beings watching the family. I instructed the woman and her two sons

2   Luke xii: 48

on the theology of angels and demons. Then I explained how the demons lose their power when we invoke the Most Holy Name of Our Lord Jesus Christ and lift our hearts in fervent prayer to the living God. I blessed the house, sprinkling water in every corner of the house, saying the antiphon, "Sprinkle me O Lord with hyssop and I shall be made clean, wash me and I shall be whiter than snow."

Then I gave the family my blessing and departed.

I kept in touch via email and another visit and continued to pray for them.

About a year later, the woman called. "Father my husband, who is rarely home since he is a truck driver, is back and we want to invite you to dinner tonight." I accepted the invitation. After dinner I asked, "So what ever happened to your house after I blessed it?"

"Father, the demons left," the woman answered. "Could you give us instructions to become Catholic?"

Of course I said yes.

And then a typical thing happened. As I was beginning instruction, the new Catechumens were hesitating.

I asked some people to pray. One seminarian scolded me for not following up better with people that I meet. I agreed and wrote him, "What are you going to do about it? Might you give me a prayer pledge?"

He pledged several Rosaries and a number of days of fasting. When I let the woman know this, she cried. She could not believe how people could do something like that for her family. They followed through with instruction and became Catholic!

I am walking in the stockyards when a couple pulls up in an SUV.

"It is a little hot," they say. "Would you like a ride?"

"Can I take a rain check? I like to walk down here in the

stockyards once in a while for a Desert Day."

"What is a Desert Day?"

"Oh, that is when I go and pray the Rosary in a place that has less traffic so I can really focus on my relationship with God. Jesus went up on a mountain to pray because there was less traffic there. I come to these stockyards for the same reason. What are your plans for the day?"

"We are going to a music festival at the south end of St. Joseph. Would you like to go?"

"Thanks for your invitation, but I have to stick with my plan to be in prayer with God today. But, for your kindness, would you like to pick out a Rosary?"

After they make their choice, I teach them how to say the "Hail Mary." They continue on to the festival and I continue with the Desert Day. Even though I came here for solitude, I do not wish to let slip away any soul whom the Lord may have sent me.

One day I decide to walk in one of St. Joseph's middle class neighborhoods. A man in his late sixties approaches me. "Do you do street preaching? I saw your article in the St. Joseph News Press."

I smile. "I do not do street preaching according to the traditional definition; meaning, I do not get on a soap box at a street corner and just start talking to myself. But if people ask me questions I answer them. If that fits the definition of street preaching, then I guess I do."

"Would you like to go to my sister's house? She really wants to meet you."

We go inside the house and he phones his sister. "You will not believe who is in your house right now. It is Father Carney!"

He hangs up the phone. "She is excited to see you."

"I can't wait to meet her." I say. "So what is your story?"

"I grew up Catholic, but I stopped going to church when I was fifteen."

"I am trying to find out why people leave the Catholic church. Would you feel comfortable sharing?"

"Oh yes. I would go to church and I would just feel physically ill. Oh, Father can you pray for me? I am going on a trip for two months to see my children. We are driving a long way."

"Certainly."

The door opens and in walks his sister. "Father, I am so happy to meet you finally. I loved reading your article about the 'Walking Priest.' Would you pray for my brother?"

"Of course, he already asked me to pray for him."

"Please pray for me, too," she asks as I am leaving. "I hope to see you all again."

Two months later a couple of seminarians ask to join me on the Rosary Walk. A man pulls up beside us and rolls down his window. "Hello Father Carney! I made it back from our trip. Thanks for the prayers."

We have a nice conversation. Before I leave, he gives me a donation. "Father, use this however you wish."

"Oh thank you!"

He tells me he works at the miniature golf course.

"When you see my car, come by and visit me."

About four months later, I am walking and see his car. I have to hold back a chuckle because I know this will be fun. I find a curb and pray the "sixth hour" of the Liturgy of the Hours. As I am about to finish, the owner of the business approaches me. "Father, do not leave. One of my relatives who works for me said he has met you before. Let me go and see if he would like to visit you."

"Great, I came here to see him." A few minutes later she comes back and leads me inside to find him.

I extend my hand to him. "Father, I would shake your hand but it is full of dirt. I am so glad you came to visit me." We catch up a little bit and I am about to leave when the owner stops me. "Father, would you like a hotdog?"

"Sure!" I sit down and talk with her while I eat. We have a nice conversation, and she says, "Father, I am so glad that I got to meet you."

After all these many months, walking, praying and meeting people, I believe what my dad tells me is true: "It is all about relationships." Being friendly, meeting people at random places, becoming a visible part of the community, sharing a meal, crossing paths. It is not only fun, but it puts people at ease with the priesthood, which may seem mysterious to many people. But there is no mystery to what I do on the streets of the city. I want people to have a part of my happiness. I am willing to share it. I am sure some people will be interested in learning how I have become so happy. Of course, God is the reason. I want people to get to know God more deeply. Eventually, I think there will be a big catch.

Photo by Jeanne Meyer

Father Carney on the Way of St James, by travel companion Elizabeth Sirba.

66 In the times and places in which, to the Church's grief, faith languished in lethargic indifference or was tormented by the baneful scourge of heresy, our great and gracious Lady, in her kindness, was ever ready with her aid and comfort.

Pope Leo XIII

4

Walking for God

I mentioned earlier that the inspiration for much of what I do began with a pilgrimage. We are all pilgrims on a journey. It is a pilgrim's heart that beats within me, and coursing through my veins is this desire to take souls with me on that journey towards God.

If you recall how I got my saturno, from that kind lady in Rome, you will remember that I was spending time traveling to determine how God wished for me to determine my vocation. On my last day in Rome, following a liturgical conference I attended, another priest and I were waiting for the train when some of the attendees of the conference saw us on the other side of the tracks. These young Polish adults were so excited to see us that they ran down the stairs across the tunnel and up the platform to talk to us. We exchanged our thoughts on the conference and then they explained how they loved to see us priests in "uniform," the saturno and the cassock.

On that evening, I began to live out of my backpack. I left the friend's house where I was staying in Rome, and took a night train to Paris. When I arrived the next morning, I walked about four miles to Montmarte, the grave site receiving the name "mount of martyrs."

Looking up from the foot of the mountain, this is a most beautiful place. The church buildings, Basilica of the Sacré-Cœur and Saint Pierre de Montmarte send out an irresistible invitation to those who love the beauty of faith.

I entered Saint Pierre de Montmarte, but I was so exhausted from carrying my heavy backpack for so long that I could not fully appreciate its beauty. I needed a place to spend the night and daylight was slipping away. As I walked out, the caretaker ran after me because he was disappointed with my short tour. He explained to me how St. Denis and his companions were beheaded on that mountain in 250 AD for preaching the Gospel in the area that later became Paris. When he was beheaded, he got up, picked up his head and walked to an appropriate place for his grave. The statue of St. Denis shows him with decapitated body carrying his head, topped by a miter, in his right hand. The caretaker showed me the gardens and a cellar where altars were set up.

This would be a great place to sleep, I thought. *I could lock the doors, sleep where the blood of the martyrs was spilled, wake up the next morning and say Mass.* I asked if I could sleep there that night. The caretaker offered me a meal and went to ask permission from the pastor for me to sleep there. Permission was not given, so I took my leave to the church across the road. In the Basilica, I saw the nave where Adoration is conducted during the night hours. Pilgrims are given very cheap lodging if they sign up for a nocturnal hour. I signed up for 5:00 AM and was given a room in the top floor of the convent. The view was breathtaking.

I woke up the next morning at five to pray in front of the Holy Sacrament of the Altar. I then made my way to London, spending three days there. After that I went north to Scotland by train, then ship. I reached Papa Stronsay Island where I visited the Transalpine Redemptorists.

Here, I spent a month discerning whether to join these zealous missionary monks. I would walk around their island, which is about one square mile, spotting seals every day and reading many collected works from St. Alphonsus de Ligouri. I decided that, due to the lack of sunlight, I could not spend the rest of my life there.

I left the island for Fontgombauldt Abbey in France to rendezvous with my friend John. We were planning to walk *el Camino de Santiago de Compostela* (The Way of St. James) in Spain, and we had decided to stay at this ancient Benedictine monastery for seven days to prepare ourselves spiritually and physically for the pilgrimage, a 500-mile journey through fields and towns and across ancient bridges, ending in Santiago, where the apostle St. James is buried. During our stay at the monastery, I would say Mass early before dawn, and John would serve, then we would eat with the guests, which numbered over twenty men.

Soon we were off to St. Jean Pied de Port for the beginning of our pilgrimage on *Camino*, known as the Way of St. James. I owe the inspiration for my *Camino* trip to John. He had served Mass when I was in a small town in Kansas. I was learning the Latin Mass, which we officially call the Extraordinary Form. Since he was well-versed in the rubrics, or rules, of the Mass, he guided me in my first months of saying the ancient form of the Mass. After I got permission to leave my parish and visit religious communities to see where I belonged, I was just about to join a community when John invited me to take some more time and discern where God was leading me. He suggested that we go on the *Camino de Santiago de Compostela.* He told me we would have to sleep on the ground since he did not have enough money to pay for lodging along the way. I said "yes."

Upon arriving, that first day in St. Jean Pied de Port, we searched for some wine, cheese, and French bread. John had killed a deer in Kansas, mixed it with one-forth hamburger meat, and dried it into long sticks. So we found a spot by the river on the edge of the city, had our meal and laid down under the stars. As I was trying to fall asleep, many thoughts rushed through my mind. I heard dogs barking in the distance and thought, *are they going to come and get us?* Then I thought, *is someone going to find us and ask us to leave?* Then I thought, *how exciting this is! I feel like an apostle!* I soon feel asleep.

Then next day I awoke and thought, *That was exciting!* I said Matins and Lauds and we began on the ancient trail to *Santiago*. It would be five hundred miles of adventure and discernment. Little did I realize how clear God would make known my vocation.

I couldn't have predicted the number of people who would want to talk to me or take a picture with me because of what I was wearing. The cassock and saturno are like magnets.

A fellow pilgrim, a woman in her forties from South Korea, first sees me in the big town of Leon. She takes pictures with me at the steps of a Cathedral.

The next time I see her is after an outdoor Latin Mass we celebrate.

"What you were doing was so beautiful," she says. "May I ask a few questions?"

She asks many things about the Mass, and we have a long discussion. A few days later she comes up to us and asks questions about my cassock and about the Catholic faith. She says she is a non-practicing Protestant. I have hope that, having seen the beauty of the faith, she will continue to seek until she finds the fullness of the truth.

We meet two German men in their early twenties. They have run out of money so I am keeping an eye on them so that they don't starve. They pitch tents in various places, like me and John. Our conversation lands on the topic of God.

"When growing up in the secular school in Germany, I got so bored in class that I went out into the hall to read the Bible," one of the young men says. "This was my real education."

"You were like a sponge thrown out into the sea," I tell him. "You soaked up the truth found in those sacred pages."

One day, I meet a forty-five year old Spanish lady from Valencia, Spain, home of the Holy Grail. She was raised Catholic, left the faith at fourteen, lived with a Protestant family in the southeastern United States as an exchange student, came back to Spain and tried to persuade Catholics to become Protestant before finally she met a holy priest who was an instrument of God and convinced her of the truth of the Catholic faith. She entered a convent, but left after a period of discernment.

Every other day or so, she talks with us about the Catholic faith. I share with her my journey and my dreams. She invites us to Valencia. After speaking with John, he and I agree to journey to southern Spain. One of my dreams was to have a dinner on the Mediterranean Sea. On our trip there, we meet some of her friends, see the Holy Grail and have that dinner on

A hay bale in north-central Spain on the Way of St. James provides a place to say Mass on a day when we could not find an available church.

Photo by Kim Young

My travel companion: John Klassen. Also pictured: Kim Young.

Photos by Kim Young

I strive for a balance between two equally important callings: being alone with God and going out and bringing God to others. This is what it means to be both contemplative and active in the religious life. St. Martin of Tours, founder of French monasticism, lived this balance. He and his men where both monks and apostles, united with God by prayer, as God called them to convert pagan people.

the sea. We have great conversations.

"The Catholic faith in Spain is dead," she says.

"God does not abandon His Church," I say. "He is raising up holy men and women who will receive graces the world has not seen for centuries. You can be a part of it if you become a woman of deep prayer."

I had no idea then that I would be having similar conversations in St. Joseph, Missouri, less than a year later. But here I am.

Five boys are playing games in the park as I walk by them. One of them spots me. He runs up to me and asks me for a Rosary. I guess I have sort of a reputation around here. I carry rosaries around and if you ask for one, I will give you one and tell you a little bit about God. As I explain how to pray the Hail Mary to nine-year-old Skyler, and what all the beads signify, his four playmates come to listen. I explain how precious the Rosary is. I ask them whether they would ask their parents to help them pray it if I gave them a prayer booklet— "How to Pray the Rosary." Each one promises. I give them each rosaries, bless the beads and continue my walk.

Three blocks later, Skyler comes running after me, calling, "Priest, priest!" His aunt wants a Rosary. We go to her house, and I bless a Rosary and give it to her.

Two of Skyler's playmates ask him, "Why did you do that?"

I tell them, "Skyler did that because he is a good boy."

I tell Skyler that God may have a special plan for him, that if he prays the Rosary, God will speak to his heart and reveal His plan. He smiles.

Nine months pass and I am speaking with a lady in a parked van. She and I are speaking about her problems. Skyler comes up next to me as I am speaking about Jesus. As I say my good-byes to the lady and start to walk again, Skyler asks if he can pray the Rosary with me. I tell him I am on my way to the Holy Rosary Credit Union down the block and that I need to have another adult with me so we can walk together.

"Father, when can you teach me about God?" he asks.

I tell him that I need him to pray that some more holy men and women join me so we can start a school. I go into the credit union to transact my business, and when I come out I see Skyler walking down the block. I watch him walk away like a lamb without a shepherd. I long for the day that God will provide a number of men and women who want to become saints and join me in finding the abandoned sheep and bringing them to the mountains to be fed; namely, the Holy Altars. "Send forth thy light and thy truth: they have conducted me, and brought me unto thy holy hill, and into thy tabernacles. And I will go in to the altar of God: to God who giveth joy to my youth" (Ps. xvii).

I walk by a bus stop and some wise guy comes up and says to me, "Hey Father, how much do they pay you to wear that hat?"

I pause for a moment to collect my thoughts, take off my saturno, scratch my head, smile, extend my hat and flip it upside down.

"I cannot wait to see," I say.

I ask Jesus to pour His Precious Blood on the men of good will in the city of St. Joseph.

I walk by a middle-aged man and his son decorating for Christmas. They are putting up a reindeer in their front yard. I smile and wave.

"Hi," he calls. "I am Bob."

"I am Fr. Carney."

After a few moments of conversation, he invites me inside. We talk for about an hour before I discover that Bob is a Missouri Synod Lutheran. As I get up from the table to leave, he offers me some tangerines.

"Bob, that is great because I am famished," I say. "All this walking has given me a great hunger."

Bob tells me to take as many tangerines as I want. He invites me to come back sometime. I am grateful for our visit and the tangerines as I continue my walk.

It is quite often the kindness of strangers that opens the door to God's grace.

A car full of young adults in their early twenties pulls up beside me as I walk.

"Aren't you hot?" one of them asks.

I respond with a smile, "Yes, but it is not bad." (I find out a few blocks later that the bank sign shows 84 degrees.)

"I do not see any sweat," a girl in the back seat says, peering out at me.

They seem to be in awe. A lady in the passenger's seat gives me some water. I tell her, with a big smile, that I am very grateful because I was just getting ready to go to the gas station to get some water. I kneel down on the sidewalk in order to be at eye level with the people in the car, open the bottle and begin to drink.

"Why do you have all those beads wrapped around your wrist?" a man from the back seat asks.

"Oh, that is so that I don't forget that I need to keep praying." I say. "Do you want to know more about the Rosary?"

They all chime in, "Yes!"

I explained how St. Dominic received the Rosary from the Blessed Virgin Mary around the thirteenth century. Some people sometimes took rose petals, dried them and put a string on them. That is why it is called a Rosary.

"Can I have one?" the driver asks.

"Sure, what is your favorite color?"

"Blue."

From my backpack, I pull out a Zip-loc bag full of a couple dozen Rosaries and spy a few blue ones.

"I think I have one you will like," I say. "Pick your

favorite out of the bag."

The other girls exclaim together, "I want one, too."

After they each pull out a Rosary, I give them a prayer pamphlet called "How to Pray the Rosary." I ask them if they would like to repeat the words the Archangel Gabriel said to the Blessed Virgin Mary. They agree. So I tell them to grip the first bead and repeat after me. We recite the Hail Mary as I pray each phrase and they repeat.

"Where do you live?" the driver asks me.

I tell him that I reside at St. James and say Mass for some nuns.

"The next time I see you, I would like to talk," the one in the back tells me.

"Certainly," I say, "here is my card."

I ask the group of young people, "How old do you think I am?"

One of them guesses 42.

"Lower," I say.

Another guesses 38. Another 39.

"Bingo."

Then I tell them, "This past year has been the happiest year of my life because I spend all my time praying and trying to unite my soul with God. Oh, I mean to say, I am not praying out loud when I sleep or eat or, you know, when I am doing other activities, like talking to you. But when I am alone with God, I constantly pray to Him and listen to Him. You see, we were created to be in union with God. And when we do that we are going to be the happiest. I am so happy. When a person is happy, he wants to spread that happiness, otherwise he will burst. So I want to spread how I have found happiness, and when I spread happiness, it makes me happier."

Four weeks later, one of those four young people finds me again, walking down the sidewalk.

"Father do you remember me?" he asks.

"You are Diego!" I exclaim. "One of the four I met a

few weeks ago. You said that you would want to talk some more."

"Yes, Father, I am at work, but I saw you and I asked my boss if I could take a break. I ran here before you got too far ahead. What are you doing Father?"

"I am walking to the hospital where someone has asked me to give a loved one the Last Rites."

"Father, I want to talk."

Since I need to get to the anointing and Diego doesn't have much time either, I try to do my best in the time we are given. I'd prefer conversation never to be rushed, so I can give each person my all. Diego and I sit on a nearby ledge and talk about some of his fellow countrymen in Mexico and their drug cartels and their murderous ways. He explains why he did not take a Rosary that day when I met him. He has been scandalized by the bad example given by the Catholics he grew up with. They have not lived virtuous lives. After I calmly explained the role of the Rosary and the Blessed Virgin Mary in leading us to holiness, I explain, "Satan wants to mimic the offering of the Sacred Blood of Jesus. The Aztecs "consecrated" a pyramid to the demon-gods in Mexico City by killing 80,000 men in four days. The 'priests' were taking out the hearts of men every fifteen seconds. Satan was being adored by the shedding of innocent human blood. The demons always draw unsuspecting mankind to worship satan by the shedding of innocent blood. He is doing that today in abortion and pharmaceutical abortion pills. Cortez destroyed the demon-gods by having a priest say the Holy Sacrifice of the Mass in a room in the pyramid. Because of his efforts, it paved the way for the coming of Our Lady of Guadalupe who was instrumental in the conversion of millions of Mexicans. Today we have to do something about abortion to pave the way for the triumph of the Immaculate Heart of Mary."

As I walk by the gas station, an old beat up car, with three young women and a child pull into the parking lot. The driver, a twenty-year-old woman covered in tattoos with an unlit cigarette hanging from her mouth, gets out of the car and looks at me.

"I see you walking all the time in town," she says. "I have always wanted to meet you, but I can never stop the car. My father has not seen you, but I tell him about you, and he does not believe me. When I tell him you wear a black robe and carry a big cross, he says that he does not think you are real." As the other two girls go into the gas station, she closes the car door behind her.

"Can we talk for a little?" she asks.

I walk over to her, smile, ask her name and shake her hand.

"I saw you reading something on a bench in the town square," she says. "I went to get my dad. When I returned to the bench it is as if you vanished. My dad still does not believe me."

"Do you want him to meet me?" I ask.

She is excited and tells me where she lives so I can pay him a visit.

"That is close to the parish of St. James where I reside," I say. "Here is my card."

The other two ladies come back with Twinkies and Ding Dongs.

"Don't you get hot wearing that outfit?" one of the women asks. "Why do you walk around all the time?"

I explain that I want to practice prayer and union with God our Creator and tell them how happy I am and how I want to give and teach this happiness to other people; I offer them each a Rosary and a blessed medal. After they pick them out, I give them a "How to Pray the Rosary" pamphlet and explain the meaning behind each medal they choose. I give them a blessing and we part company with a smile.

It is not long before another small act of kindness opens the flood gates of God's grace.

I walk along the sidewalk, and a woman comes to me with water and bottle of Gatorade.

"Man of God, do you remember me?" she asks.

I most certainly do. I remember clearly that, in my first weeks of the Rosary walks in St. Joseph, a young lady pulled up to me as I crossed the driveway of a CVS pharmacy.

"You look like a man of God," she had said. "Do you need a ride?"

"Thank you for the offer, but I love walking," I responded. "What is your name?"

"Angela."

I said, "Oh, Angela, a name with the root word "Angel," which means 'messenger.' You may have been sent by God to give me that beautiful message when you said, 'You look like a man of God.' May I pray for you?"

She smiled and said, "Of course."

Another car was behind hers, so I told her, "You probably have to go since people are waiting, but I hope I get to see you again."

Now, a year later, here she is.

"I have seen you walking all over town throughout this year, and I always want to offer you a ride, but you like to walk so I never stop to offer. But today I saw you and I wanted to talk to you. Would you like water or Gatorade?"

"Oh, you are so kind," I say, looking at the cold drinks. "I will drink water."

We enjoy a long conversation about personal problems, religious dreams and my plans for the Rosary walks and a community of men and women who propagate the faith in the cities.

"Father, when you walk by, people are so blessed to see you praying and giving us a good example," she tells me. Then she asks if I am on Facebook.

"No, I just cannot spend the time on that. I like to meet people face to face. Then I can really communicate with them and give them sacramentals. Would you like a Rosary?"

She asks me what a Rosary is. I explain and she accepts

my offer. I let her pick one out.

"Father, I do not know how to explain it," she says, "but when you walk by, it is as if you have spiritual ribbons that peel off your garment and they are left behind to bring joy and happiness along the path you trod."

I explain my secret. "Oh Angela, let me tell you what is happening. Can I show you something?" I pull out some CD's from the Benedictines of Mary, Queen of the Apostles. "You see these Nuns? Look at their beautiful faces."

She grabs one of the CDs and looks intently at their pictures.

I continue, "They are contemplatives. They are Spouses of Jesus Christ. Have you heard of the nine choirs of angels?"

"No."

"OK. Starting from bottom to top, we have angels, archangels, virtues, powers, principalities, dominations, thrones, cherubim and seraphim. These angels are sometimes grouped into subcategories. The first three mentioned provide assistance with human beings on a more or less individual basis. The next three assist us more in general, watching over nations, and parishes. The last three are closest to God; the cherubim and seraphim are so close to God that they are depicted in Christian art by being on fire, the fire of God that does not consume, but gives life. These are kind of like the Nuns who go to choir in the chapel where God dwells at least nine times a day to sing His praises. Since I am their chaplain, their priest and father, I ask them to pray in front of the Altar of God on behalf of the people I meet when I do the Rosary walks. So, Angela, they have been praying for you for over a year now!"

She is so thrilled that she wants to hear more, but it is getting late. I tell her to stop me again sometime, and I give her my blessing and go my way.

"My Catholic sons and brothers, we can only build a certain foundation for masculinity on the rock, Jesus Christ. We look to our Savior to be transformed in Him, to be the men we are called to be, and to let others see Him in us.

The Most Rev. Thomas J. Olmsted,
Bishop of Phoenix

5

Carrying the Cross

I love the sun, but sometimes in St. Joseph, it can be a little brutal for a man clothed in black from head to toe. Sometimes, along my walks, I stop for a tea break. Not the kind you might be picturing. Not at a parlor with fancy table linens and china teapots. My tea breaks are much different. I go into a gas station or a fast food restaurant and ask, "How much does it cost for hot water and ice in my cup?" Ninety-nine times out of a hundred the response is "free." So I take a half cup of hot water and drop in a tea bag from my backpack. Usually as I am brewing the tea, someone will come up and chat. Many times these chats turn into talks about God and religion. After brewing, I trash the tea bag and fill the cup up with ice. Unless it is cold out. Then I just drink it hot. I especially like to have a slice of lemon, if there is any around.

So, I am enjoying my tea outside the gas station, leaning on a propane cage that serves as my bar. I place my Crucifix and Breviary on it. A middle-aged mother, Cindy, and her daughter, Heather, who looks like she is in her mid-twenties, come up to me.

"Father, would it bother you to chat?" the mother asks.

"Of course not," I say.

Come to find out, her daughter works behind the counter of the gas station.

"Your daughter always has a smile and is willing to give me free hot water and ice," I say to the woman.

As the conversation progresses, the mother reveals her Catholic upbringing and the reasons why she left the practice of the faith. It just so happens that she has a load of old Catholic sacramentals and books with her that she is getting ready to donate to a Catholic Bookstore in town. She asks if I want to see them. It is like inviting a child into a candy store and telling him that he can pick whatever he wants. I am thrilled to find a pamphlet of the Litany of St. Philomena written by St. John Marie Vianney. I take that pamphlet and a few other prayer cards with me. I have a special devotion to St. Philomena, and I will tell you why later.

The woman's daughter gives me her business card. She makes jewelry and rosaries.

Several months later, I give her a call to fix my broken Rosary beads. We meet at a coffee shop called "Cafè Pony Espresso," named after the Pony Express which began in St. Joseph, Missouri. She brings her mother and brother with her and fixes my Rosary right there on the spot as we talk.

Three months after that, two of my rosaries break, so I will call her again. She speaks about some family problems. Then we talk some philosophy and theology.

The story is yet unfinished. Like most of the stories started on the streets where I walk. But my hope for them is that our meeting is the beginning of many good things to come.

I spend quite a bit of time at the local soup kitchen. The volunteers like it when I come in. Sometimes they say, "Father we have not seen you for a while." One day I am waiting in line for coffee when a lady surrounded by her daughters and grandchildren asks, "What are you?"

"I am a Catholic Priest."

"What do they call you?"

"Father."

"Boy, you have really big feet."

I look down at my feet and back at her and just put my hands up and smile. She invites me to her table, so I get my coffee and join her.

I take out my bag of Rosaries and sacramentals. Scores of people gather around the table as I explain how to pray the Rosary. Not everyone wants a Rosary, but many do. I also give away a few sacred medals, explaining the meaning behind each one.

It is time for me to leave since my brother and his family are parked outside. They have come up from Kansas City to the Pumpkin Festival. As I am leaving, three groups of people stop me in the parking lot, wanting to talk. One is concerned about a family issue that they want me to pray for; another tells me a short life story; and the last is someone who wants a Rosary and wants to know how to pray. When I finally get to my brother and his wife and kids, they tell me I am a magnet.

"Is this neat or what?" I say exuberantly.

My family and I walk over to a nearby restaurant and have a meal together. As we are leaving, we learn that one of the people whom I had met on the sidewalk apparently paid our bill!

It's a new day now and I walk into Hardees for a tea break. I get some hot water from the counter, set my cup on the table and drop in a tea bag to brew. A middle-aged woman comes up to me.

"I saw your article in the St. Joseph News Press last

year," she says. "Do you talk about spiritual things?"

I smile and say, "Of course."

We talk for almost an hour. She has just gotten out of an abusive relationship. She stopped attending the Catholic Church over two years ago. Her daughter, a freshman in high school, comes over to the table with her boyfriend. The mother explains how both sets of parents agree to them seeing each other, but since they are so young, they should never be alone.

"I commend you for courting," I tell the young couple. "Courting means that the couple abstains from physical intimacy. It gives them a chance to know the family because they are always around. It is very traditional to court and it has many benefits."

I turn to the young man and tell him, "Society teaches men something bad. Our fallen culture glamorizes promiscuity. We wrongly say that he is a man for getting these women. But I say to you, we need to return to virtue. The word "virtue" comes from the Latin root, "vir," which means "man." Virtue means one thinks good thoughts, says good things, and practices good actions on a habitual basis. When a man gives into temptation, he is not acting manly or virtuous, but he is weak. Women who have the use of their reason are looking for virtuous men to marry. If you give into temptation, eventually it will ruin your life, and it could be the cause of your eternal damnation."

"I used to be an investment analyst and I managed $200 million. When we invest money now for a gain in the future, at the end there is usually a big payoff. Life requires an investment. For example to forgo pleasure now so that you will not get someone pregnant or pick up a sexually transmitted disease. If you become a virtuous man, good women who respect your virtue and don't seek to take it away will become candidates for your future marriage. You will be esteemed by women of good virtue."

"I know this is hard to hear. If you endure what I say and follow it, there will be a big payoff. Just like investing money in the stock market, which provides a large return for the wise man. Investing in virtue and putting off pleasure now will provide great happiness in the future."

"And now that I ruined your day, I must be going." I smile.

My "parishioners" give me a smile in return and thank me for my time and efforts.

"Now I think God wants me to start going to Mass and Confession," the mother says.

I give them a blessing before I leave.

As I walk down the street, a young man gets out of his car and introduces himself to me. He has a little boy with him. He says he infrequently attends Mass. He tells me about his busy life, working at a hospital and raising his little boy. I sense that the man is ready to hear a little preaching, so I let him have it.

"You have a saintly priest in your parish. If I were you I would go and ask him for spiritual guidance like Mary, who sat at the feet of Jesus. She chose the best part.

After, he explains how he got a woman pregnant out of wedlock and is left to raise the boy on his own, I challenge him with the same talk I gave to that teenage boy back at Hardees – that of being a virtuous man and not giving into temptation.

Then smiling, I look him in the face, and after a brief pause I ask, "What is your goal in life?"

After stumbling over his words without really giving an answer, I give him mine: "Our goal should be to become saints."

I speak to him of the many saints who fathered a child without the benefit of a sacramental marriage, but still rose to become great people in the eyes of God. Among them was St. Augustine.

As I deliver this message, I am moving my arms like an Italian, sometimes jumping up and down to get a point across, and overall on fire with the love of God and the desire to share my happiness.

I give him my blessing, and we depart.

Two months later, my friend, the priest who I suggested the man go see, takes me to lunch at a local pizza joint. The owners of the pizza shop are the parents of the man I talked to about pursuing sainthood after living a less than perfect life. My priest friend introduces me to the owners.

"Father, my son was really impressed with what you said," the woman tells me.

I explain how I am always so happy to talk about the joy of the Gospel, and I hope that I had not been too forceful.

"Father, you made a positive impression on my son," the father says.

I explain how I believe we need to revive the religious orders of priests who walk the streets and give missions.

There was a time when orders of priests used to give missions in cities where they were invited. A missionary community would stay at a parish for two weeks. The first week they would travel around the city, two by two in their habits, praying the Rosary for the city's conversion. When these men were approached, they would speak about and hand out fliers for the mission that they would be giving in the local parish the following week. The city couldn't help but take note of eight, ten or even more than a dozen men walking around town, praying. People's curiosity would be stoked.

You are probably getting the idea by now that my vision is a bit bigger than just one priest walking around praying the Rosary in one town. Some day, through the order I envision, I would like to get permission from bishops in every diocese to allow what happens in St. Joseph to happen all over the world. It's a big dream. But it's not bigger than God's grace. And if He wills it, and I remain devoted, I have no doubt that the vision that St. Louis de Montfort set forth in the book I read as I crossed the street that Providential day a year ago just might come to pass. *"They shall carry...the Crucifix in their right hand, the Rosary in their left..."*

Photo by Steven Bateson

" The soul that seeks recreation outside of the Creator, and consolation outside of Christ, will never find them.

St. Philip Neri

6

A Gift of Real Estate from the Blessed Mother

The best part about making the arduous pilgrimage *El Camino de Santiago* is its completion, which is like a foretaste of heaven. The pilgrims arrive there all sweaty and hungry. They go into the Basilica of St. James and offer worship and thanksgiving to God. Outside, pilgrims gather and share food and stories of perseverance. There is a sense of camaraderie, a satisfaction that "we did this together."

Sometimes we don't have a living concept of heaven, which is the destination of our whole earthly pilgrimage. We may even see an eternal life of gazing upon God as something boring. But in heaven, we will see ourselves as God sees us. He is our Creator and Father, and He finds great beauty in us. We will also experience others as God sees them and fully recognize their beauty. Since nothing in heaven is tainted, all of our sins and defects will have been purged. Then, in the Beatific Vision, we will have the greatest joy as we see God

Himself. Yet this infinite bliss is not a mere staring for we will see and experience God reflected in ourselves and in each other as He lives in us! We will never be bored in heaven. It will be like infinite beginnings, and we will explore. We'll say, "Wow!" And then again, right away, "Wow!"

In St. Joseph, there is a beautiful Gothic Revival church. It is so grand, its two spires can be seen from twelve miles away, across the Missouri river from the Kansas side. Outside the church, there is a beautiful statue of the Blessed Virgin Mary depicted as the Immaculate Conception. The first time I see it, I think, "I need to go make a holy hour." As I enter the crypt, I hear two little beeps. "Oh we are closing her up," the janitor says. "I am turning off the water. We are putting this church up for sale."

"You mean this is not a Catholic church?" I ask.

"No. The Diocese got rid of it a few decades ago. Recently, it has been used as a wedding chapel."

"What a shame. May I have a look?"

"Go ahead."

I carefully open the beautiful wooden door and walk up some winding stairs. The first thing I notice were the frosty, wavy glass windows, formed by that artistic design called the "camel's needle point." Once I enter the vestibule, I open the doors and think, "Wow!"

Although the church has not been maintained perfectly, it has so many beautiful Catholic treasures, that I have to pause for a moment and catch my breath. I feel like I have walked into a European Church. There is a Gothic high altar and two side altars filled with old saints. The stained glass windows depicting twelve scenes from the life of the Blessed Virgin Mary are so captivating. I find out later they were made in Austria, and they rival some of the most beautiful stained glass windows of the great cathedrals of the United States, including the Cathedral of the Immaculate Conception, in Wichita, Kansas, where I was ordained a priest.

As I walk out, the janitor asks me, "Do you want the business card of the owner? They are putting this church up for sale."

"No," I say, "I have no way to buy it."

Back outside, I can't take my eyes off the church. I am in awe of the great dedication of the builders and the faith of the people who built it. The cornerstone bears these words, "Conceptio Immacula, 1908."

As I walk away I remember a priest I knew who taught me that it is efficacious to make the sign of a cross over any structures you want to claim for Christ. So from that day forward, I make the sign of the cross over the old church any chance I get. I have visions of saying Mass in the Extraordinary Form there, drawing people in off the streets to see the beauty of ancient liturgy and having monks chant sacred music at various times of the day, luring weary sinners in with irresistible beauty, making them hungry for something that surpasses all earthly pleasures—the beauty and truth of God.

As time goes on, it becomes a habit for me to ask the Blessed Virgin Mary, "If you want this church back into Catholic hands, just let me have it." That is my frequent prayer.

Then on August 5th, the Dedication of the Church of Our Lady of the Snows, I put out a prayer request to the 140 prayer warriors who pray for my mission.

In my Breviary, I read these words about how "On the 5th of August, which is always the season of the greatest heat in the City [Rome], snow fell by night and covered part of the Esquiline hill. And on that same night, the Mother of God told a man named John and his wife separately in dreams that they should build a church on that place. When John told this to Pope Liberius, he said that he had the same dream. The Pope therefore went to the snow-covered hill and there marked out the site." (*Breviarium Romanum*, August 5th).

I write to the prayer warriors, telling them this story,

and adding, "Now I want to ask you to pray for a miracle on this day, that if the Blessed Virgin Mary wants us to have this church that she give it to us."

I speak to the bishop about the church and he encourages me to speak with the former pastor, who is a retired priest still living in the city. I draft a letter to the owners who live in Canada. The summary of the letter was the question, "For the love of God, would you give me your church?"

A number of months later, a prayer warrior from Baton Rouge, Louisiana, brings his family to Kansas City for a wedding. He calls me up with a question: "Could we come up to St. Joseph to see that church?"

"Yes," I say, "but I am supposed to keep quiet about it."

He looks at the outside of the church, but we can't go inside because it is all locked up. After five minutes, he declares, "We are going to buy it."

So on January 6th, the Solemnity of the Epiphany, the man and his friends purchased the church.

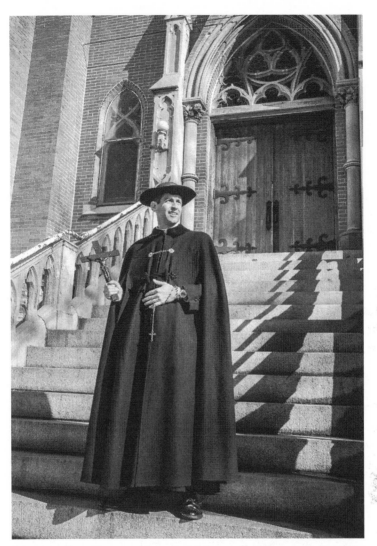

Immaculate Conception, Saint Joseph, Missouri. Built in 1908, this Catholic Cathedral was slated for demolition in 1994, but saved by the Catholic faithful who wanted it preserved. It was used as a nondenominational wedding chapel before being closed down and then finally recaptured by Catholics 2015.

Photos by Steven Bateson
St. Joseph, Missouri

"The very fact that God has placed a certain soul in our way is a sign that God wants us to do something for him or her.

St. Mother Teresa

7

Providence at Work

As I mentioned earlier, sometimes I like to go on a "Desert Walk." I go on these walks, in sparsely populated areas, to be more alone with God. In St. Joseph, Missouri, the area I choose for this is called "The Stockyards." Many decades ago, they used to slaughter cattle in those yards. Today they slaughter pigs. The area is considered an industrial zone with all the typical uninspiring buildings, water treatment facilities, grain elevators, stockyards, and about a dozen factories or so. I go here to get away because, strangely, it is an oasis of solitude.

This area is in sharp contrast to downtown St. Joseph, with its old churches, commercial fronts and historic mansions and residential areas. South St. Joseph has its industry, its rail roads and quaint residential areas, nestled among lots of greenery. The east side of town has old, well-kept residential areas, hospitals, a university and a number of high schools. North St. Joseph has "Lover's Lane," a popular and scenic road scattered with houses tucked in among the rolling, hillside preserve. To the west is the Missouri River, separating Kansas from Missouri.

I am in "the desert'" on a day when a young 20-year-old is parking at the end of the sidewalk.

"Father, do you need a ride?" he asks.

We launch into an hour-long conversation. I listen to his life story. We talk about topics like methamphetamine drugs and the sad lives of the people that work at the factories who are deep in the drug life. We talk about religious topics too.

After we go our separate ways, I think to myself, "These encounters have so many positive effects. The Church meets people that may have never approached Her. These Rosary walks I do interest people at an age where they are still open to learning how to find happiness in a culture that predominately gives them discouragement. These encounters are based on Divine Providence and are not planned; therefore, in my observation they are fun from both sides of view. The ones who come up to me are curious to know what I am about or they are hungry to find God and they are drawn to me. From my point of view, it is so simple and effective. When I am walking, I am praying, listening to God in the desert of the cities. Then when someone approaches, I have a chance to listen and sometimes give them the fruits of my contemplation. I love this. I want to teach other people this happiness I have found. I have never been happier in my life. I feel that if I did not share my happiness with other people, I would explode. These encounters are so real, meaning they will have a direct effect on our eternity. We do not do well to just try to get to heaven on our own. We need to bring people with us!

I find a tan Vel-cro wallet as I am walking along the shoulder of the road in the stockyards. I pick it up and am surprised to find a driver's license of a twenty-two year old, a $10 bill and a $1 bill. A few days later, after looking at the address on a map, I take a walk to the address on the driver's license. A very old man across the street sits on his front porch.

I say hello and introduce myself before opening the gate and knocking on the door of the wallet's owner. An old lady cracks the door open about six inches and peers out.

"Do you know James Clark?" I ask.

"Oh yes," she says, "he is my grandson."

"I found his wallet in the stockyards," I say.

She opens the door. "Come on in," she says. "My grandson is not here, but would you like to speak to his dad?"

"Yes."

In a minute, a man in his late forties appears. His face betrays his alarm. I smile and extend my hand. "I am Fr. Carney. I found your son's wallet in the stockyards."

I hand it to him, and he looks inside, takes out the $11 and holds it out to me saying, "I do not hear of this happening any more, where people return a wallet with all the money. May I give this cash to you?"

I put up my hands, "No thank you. My treasure is with God. Just tell your son that perhaps God is trying to tell him something; namely, a priest finding his wallet and returning it to him. You will all be in my prayers."

I take down their names, shake the father's hand and am about to leave when I notice tears welling up in the father's eyes. After I resume my walk, I cannot help but think, "God, you sure are good at making divine meetings." The Rosary walks allow for a slower pace and the time to do small things for God. I am sure God will do a lot of work with this encounter. I am convinced that the Rosary walks are about meeting people and leaving them in a position where they want to see and come up to you again. It is important to keep the encounters short so they desire to continue the conversation. I tell people that the Rosary walks can be compared to a pond on a calm day. Imagine a pond with no ripples, one where you can see your reflection. The Rosary walks can be compared to dropping little pebbles in all different areas of the pond. The smooth ripples go in every direction. When the priest does kind acts and leaves the people better off than when he found them, people talk. They think, "Hey that priest did this good thing or that good thing." Word gets around fast. Once the priest has secured a sound reputation, then he has gained the confidence of the people. But we cannot forget that having an army of nuns praying for you is a special bonus!

I meet Justin on a bridge over Interstate 29 on the edge of Western Missouri State University in St. Joseph. He is in his mid-20s. He offers me a ride, which I am glad to take. I ask him if he has time to give me a tour of the university since he is a recent graduate. After driving me around, we go to his place of work, a juvenile detention center. The place is full of troubles. He tells me all about it. I ask him, "Would you like me to give a blessing to the place?" He gladly accepts. After the blessing, he takes me back into town because I need to get back to the Cathedral. Along the way we talk about serving at the Holy Sacrifice of the Altar. He explains how he loved to serve at Mass. He tells me some personal problems, then we enter the Cathedral and pray a few prayers to put his issues in the Hand of God.

I have no way of knowing that a year from then, as I go walking in the stockyards, the gas station will be closed so I will have to go next door to the animal shelter for some water and a place to cool down. As I'm sitting in the waiting room, Justin and his girl friend will walk in. We are happy to see each other. Justin explains how his dad is a fan of the Rosary walks.

"My dad really likes what you are doing. He thinks we need to do more of that."

After a good conversation, I depart on my walk.

The random follow-ups are important because the element of Divine Providence is at work. People say over and over to me, "Father, I do not believe in coincidence, but in Providence." Providence is defined by some theologians as a sister virtue of Prudence. Prudence is that virtue that helps us discern how to do what is right, at the right time, in the right way. This is complimentary with Providence, placing our confidence in God's timing and His work. We still must do the duties of our state in life, but when we place ourselves in the Hand of God, He is working. Providence is clearly demonstrated by these encounters with people at places and times when their souls are open to seeing the work of God. Part of what makes the connections exciting is how one meets people. The Rosary walks bring the sacred into the world.

> **"When I am walking, I am praying, listening to God in the desert of the cities. Then when someone approaches, I have a chance to listen and sometimes give them the fruits of my contemplation. I love this. I want to teach other people this happiness I have found. I feel that if I did not share my happiness with other people, I would explode."**

Providence guides my every step since I have taken to the street to pray. It was providential that the local newspaper wrote an article on the Rosary walks, which eventually led to my publisher asking me to write this book. It was an article that almost never existed. The *St. Joseph News Press* contacted the priest whom I was living with, and he gave me the contact information for reporter Jana Sauber. I told the priest that I do not trust the media, but he encouraged me. Once the article was published, it also made it to the internet in electronic form. Someone had gotten that article and sent it to their friends and it got around. Months later people continue to share it on the internet.

This is the important lesson I am learning. In the past, I would have imprudently pushed the article around to my friends to distribute it. But I was inspired to pray for providence. I begged God to get this article seen by many if it would be for the salvation of souls and for my sanctification.

He answered my prayer. The article got around. I realized this did not fuel my pride as it would have done if I were to have spread the article myself. Instead it was an answer to prayer. I saw that God was responsible since it was not accomplished by my efforts. This humbled me.

Another thing I was praying for was that God would find a way for me to write a book about the Rosary walks and have it published. This is one of the small ways to answer the popes' call to promote a "New Evangelization." If I had done it my way, I would have written a book and tried to publish it myself. But my past experiences have shown me that this would only lead to a failure on my part. So, I prayed to God that His Providence would take over. I trusted that if writing a book would lead to the salvation of souls and my personal sanctification, then God would make it happen. Months after the newspaper article was written, a Catholic book publisher was scrolling through her Facebook feeds, something she rarely does, and saw the somewhat dated article about me that one of her friends had shared. She contacted Mother Cecilia of the Benedictines of Mary in order to reach me. And that is why you are reading this book.

Since God is the God of Hosts, as we say in the *Sanctus*, the "Holy, holy, holy..." before the prayers of consecration of the Mass, once He gets behind a project, it just takes off! And, oh what fun it becomes!

Photo by Jeanne Meyer

Photos by Steven Bateson
St. Joseph, Missouri

Photo by Steven Bateson
St. Joseph, Missouri

Photo by Steven Bateson
St. Joseph, Missouri

Photo by Steven Bateson
St. Joseph, Missouri

Photo by Steven Bateson

"The history of the Rosary shows how this prayer was used in particular by Dominicans at a difficult time for the Church due to the spread of heresy. Today we are facing new challenges. Why should we not once more have recourse to the Rosary, with the same faith as those who have gone before us? The Rosary retains all its power and continues to be a valuable pastoral resource for every good evangelizer.

St. John Paul II

8

I Preach the Rosary

If I ever need a reason to smile, I go to the soup kitchen. One day, as I am about to enter the "Open Door Food Pantry," I notice some kids peeking through the window at me. As soon as I get inside, two of them come up to me—five-year-old Hannah and her nine-year-old sister Ashliegh.

"I want one of those Rosaries," the younger one says.

"I want a Rosary," echoes the older one.

They continue talking so I sit down in the nearest chair to listen to what they have to say. Mostly, it's a lot of questions.

"What is that black robe you are wearing?" one of them asks.

"It is a cassock."

"Can we touch your hat? What is it called?"

I look to their mother for permission, and she approves.

"The hat is called a saturno," I say, "for Saturn, the planet. See?" I put it back on my head and explain the sphere of Saturn and the "dish" around it.

I turn to the children's mother.

"May I have your permission to hand out Rosaries?"

She smiles and gives her approval.

I ask the younger girl, "Could you try to answer a question before I give you a Rosary?"

"Why?"

"It is important to know about God when you receive your Rosary. How many persons are in the Trinity?"

She is confused so I say, "Make the sign of the Cross with me. In the Name of the Father, and of the Son and of the Holy Spirit." I continue, "How many persons are in the Trinity?"

She still cannot answer, so I tell her she can ask someone for help. Her mother says, "God the Father, God the Son and God the Holy Spirit."

She still needs help, so Ashliegh whispers in her ear.

"Three!" Hannah finally says.

I give her a Rosary, which makes her very happy since she "passed the test."

I notice another girl watching from a distance.

"Oh, she is shy," Ashliegh explains. "Can I have a Rosary?"

"Can you tell me one of the three persons in the Trinity?"

She can't come up with the answer so her mother says, "Father!"

"Father," Ashliegh echoes.

I give her a Rosary and pamphlet.

I look at the girl who is shy. "Do you want to play Catholic trivia, too?"

She nods.

"First, what is your name?"

She comes toward me. "Mercedes."

"How old are you?"

"Seven."

I point at my Crucifix on the table and ask, "Can you tell me the name of the person on the cross?"

"Jesus!" she exclaims.

"What is your favorite color?"

She picks out a Rosary and asks for a pamphlet to go with it.

As the girls and their caregivers have to leave, another group of women come and put down their food trays and begin to talk about their troubles. One of them, named Sherri, says, "It is good to get your problems out. Otherwise, it will make you sick." She asks for my contact information before we part ways, and I give her my card.

I think it sets a good example and encourages others when a priest becomes friends of those "less fortunate." This is true on a spiritual level as well as a material level. As the word gets around that a priest is hanging out with those in need, people of good will take note, and their faith is strengthened as well in the supernatural character of the church and the priesthood. There are many organizations that feed the hungry, clothe the naked and house the homeless, but it is good when we are ever mindful that our deeper spiritual hunger needs attention as well. "Do not search for food that perishes, but food that will remain unto eternal life" (Jn, vi: 27).

Some people ask me, "What do you preach?"

I tell them that I preach the Rosary. Rosaries are beautiful. People place Rosaries in prominent places. People often remember who gave them a Rosary. They remember the simple things taught when they received the Rosary. It is a sacramental and has a mysterious way of drawing people to God. It is no wonder St. Dominic, by means of the Rosary, crushed heresy. The Blessed Virgin Mary illuminates all truth. A certain heresy termed "modernism" by Pope Pius X leads many astray in our times. It can be summed up in one sentence: "Out with the old, and in with the new." Modernism pushes an agenda that newer is always better. Old devotions and practices

85

are dismissed casually, without good reason, simply because of the phrase, "We do not do that anymore." Or phrases like "The cassock is a dress," or "the Mass is only a meal to share and not a sacrifice." Or priests are criticized for upholding the moral teachings of the Church, as though such teachings are uncharitable, and "we now have a kinder, gentler Church." Although it is a struggle for fallen human nature to adhere to the moral law, this struggle is the only path to freedom and the fulfillment of the human heart - as Jesus Himself said very clearly, "the truth will set you free."

It seems the Rosary could very well crush the modernist heresy. After walking thirty-two days on the *Camino* in Spain, sleeping on the ground, and travelling five hundred miles on foot, I realized how valuable walking and praying the Rosary is for propagating the faith. Some people have written or told me that the cassock is a barrier to evangelization, but John and I did a study on the *Camino*. I wore the cassock every day, and we took note that around one thousand people made contact with us by asking to take our picture or to talk with us. I concluded that the cassock is not a barrier, but a bridge.

While backpacking in Europe, wearing my cassock, saturno and Rosary beads, I could not help but notice the droves of people who approached. Then it came to me. During my time of discernment, I was inspired to gather some men and walk around the city of St. Joseph. With this inspiration, Mother Cecilia suggested the possibility of a new foundation of men, a new community. Now a more concrete vision began to grow out of that idea. We could be canons regular at home and apostles abroad. With the help of the nuns, who are gifted musicians, we could learn to chant the Divine Office Roman style in the morning and evenings, and walk around spreading devotion to the Rosary in the afternoons. We would need a monastery in the middle of the city where people could walk into the church while the Holy Sacrifice of the Mass is celebrated and Gregorian Chant is prayed from the Roman Breviary.

I am walking one day in a rundown part of St. Joseph. A young man says hello from his front door. He motions for me to come over.

"How are you?" he asks.

"Better than ever!" I reply.

"What are you?"

"I am a Catholic missionary priest."

"Do you want a Pepsi?"

"Certainly."

He leaves and comes back out with his four kids and the Pepsi.

"Thank you," I say, opening the can. "What is your name?"

"Justin," he replies.

The kids look at me shyly and then begin to ask questions: "Dad why does that man wear that?"

Justin speaks gently to his kids: "Ask him."

The kids just look at me. Finally one of them gets up the courage to ask, "Why do you wear that?"

"This shows people that I pray to God," I tell him. "God made us, and He wants us to live with Him forever. We will have fun and be happy with God forever. But first we have to be good. I am a priest and I try to show people the path to God. The devil is evil and does not want us to be with God. He does not want us to be happy. He is bad."

After our brief conversation, I ask Justin, if I can trace the sign of the cross on his forehead and the children's foreheads. He says yes. I start with the father and oldest child, and then the others become eager. "I want that, too," they say. So I happily oblige. As I trace the blessing, I pray that they find the path to God.

A little later in the day, a few blocks from Justin's house, I am waiting for a light to change when a man speaks to me from his truck. He tells me his name is Dave and asks, "Why do you wear that?"

"I wear this so I can encourage people to talk to me about God."

The light turns and he says, "God Bless."

I take my cross and bless him with the sign of the cross.

Things like these happen all the time, too numerous to include in this book. People honk, wave, smile, make a greeting, come up to me just to say 'hello.' I don't usually come to know the rest of the story with these people. But I am excited that some day I will see the effect I had on these people, after this life, when I see Jesus face to face. When all the souls and bodies of mankind will come together to see Christ the King seated in judgment, I cannot wait to see all the people whom I met as a priest. I am sure that the presence of a priest, out on the streets, walking and spreading the joy of the Gospel, will have many positive effects on people's lives. On that day, I will also see how many people have been praying for me and making my mission possible.

People are curious about the women who spend their lives hidden in prayer in the countryside of Gower at the Priory of Our Lady of Ephesus. They follow the Rule of St. Benedict, a simple life of *ora et labora*, prayer and work. They sing Gregorian Chant during the Divine Office nine times a day, singing all 150 Psalms every week. Their pure singing voices at Holy Mass pierce to the heart all who approach the Divine Mysteries, and there are testimonies of people who converted to the Faith because of hearing their music CDs. The nuns also sew beautiful, customized vestments for priests. They have a retreat house for priests and seminarians, and they serve home-cooked meals to their guests and their chaplain. That means that sometimes I get served fresh milk and homemade ice cream from their cows! The sisters' other daily work includes tending their garden and orchard and taking care of the monastery.

In the beginning, God set His eyes upon Adam and Eve's hearts, and He continues to create human beings to be in union with Him. Every human soul is of great value, and God calls some to be entirely His even in this life. If we were to see a human soul in the state of Sanctifying Grace, we would think she was an angel. But in Jesus Christ, who took on human flesh, God chooses humans for spouses, not angels! Women who become nuns are called by God in an intimate way to a spiritual marriage with Jesus. Faith is the ring worn by a true spouse of Christ who knows her husband is the King of Heaven. I have asked women in my sermons, Would you like to marry a monarch or a peasant? What would you say if the King of Heaven proposed to you?"

These consecrated women are called away from their families to live in community together. The sisters who have made solemn vows commit their lives to remain within the monastery and don't ordinarily leave the grounds. The sisters come from various backgrounds. Half the battle is entering the convent because it means sacrificing much and surrendering to a life of faith. But God is our joy. The spiritual life should be sweet and easy. We just get knocked off course by so many lies in the world. Every person is called to foster union with God through time in contemplation. Those who are privileged with a vocation to center their lives radically on God and contemplate Him have a great spiritual advantage, which is a gift for the whole Church. Contemplatives realize an eternal value in themselves and zeal for their own souls becomes zeal for all souls. This is where the nuns' mission is joined to mine. By their prayers, contemplatives invite God to open hearts.

Their monastery is called the Priory of Our Lady of Ephesus because Ephesus is where the Blessed Virgin Mary lived with St. John the Beloved after Our Lord's Ascension into heaven. Other Apostles would have visited Mary there as well, and the nuns especially try to model this part of the life of Mary. As Mary, Queen of Apostles, encouraged her Son's successors to extend the Kingdom of God through His Church, so these contemplative women offer loving support as they spur on the apostles of our times: bishops, priests, seminarians and missionaries. They inspire me to be bold and to go out into the deep for a big catch.

Often people come up to me and say, "Father, I saw you at such and such place." Or, "Father remember me when I said this or that?" After those initial greetings, the "ice breakers," so to speak, we have a substantial conversation about the truth and the afterlife.

One day, a mother of five stops her van at the corner as I cross the street. The eldest daughter says, "all the children need to be baptized."

The mother interrupts. "I almost became a nun, but they stopped wearing the habit and I stopped going to church many years ago. I like what you are wearing. I saw priests wear that back then. Could you explain it to us?"

"Yes, this is a cassock. Decades ago priests had to wear this in public, for the most part. The hat is called a *capillo romano,* a word in Italian for 'Roman hat.' (It is also called a saturno.) This is a sacred cassock because it is blessed and it is sprinkled with holy water. In my observation, it has a supernatural draw to people that have good hearts. I put it on because I am a priest and because I want to draw people to God through his supernatural grace. I think baptizing your children will help your family because they will be filled with supernatural grace, namely, the life of God."

She smiles. "We need to do that."

I give her a parish bulletin, and we say our goodbyes as she drives off.

Let me give the reason for my hope that renewing Catholic life in America really is possible. It is Mary! In *True*

Devotion to Mary, St. Louis de Montfort prophecies a time of great sanctity within a flourishing Church. His conviction stems from one foundational virtue of the Blessed Virgin: "Mary was singularly hidden during her life...Her humility was so profound that she had no inclination on earth more powerful or more constant than that of hiding herself, from herself, as well as from every other creature, so as to know God only." He explains that it was necessary for Mary to be hidden in the early days of Christianity when people would have been too easily attached to her without the necessary prior understanding of Our Lord Jesus Christ as fully God and fully Man. But now this reason for hiding Mary exists no longer.

"The most holy Virgin Mary, who brought Him into the world for the first time...will make His second advent full of splendor." She will shine in mercy "to bring back and lovingly receive the poor strayed sinners who shall be converted and shall return to the Catholic Church."

One day a young grandmother and her seven-year-old grandson pull up beside me in a Volkswagen beetle as I am walking along the sidewalk.

"Are you the 'Walking Priest' from the *St. Joseph News-Press*?" she asks.

"Yes that is me."

"Do you make home visits?"

"Of course."

And with that, I receive an invitation to her home, which was right down the block.

It is a very nice house in an affluent part of St. Joseph.

"I read your article, and I think what you are doing is great," she says. She serves some tea and speaks about things that had gone wrong in her former church.

"Sinners are in the church," I tell her, "including our Catholic Church. But do not let them get in between you and Jesus."

We continue a brief conversation about God and the

world. We agree that our society is crumbling. Before I leave, I give the woman and her grandchild each a Rosary and teach them how to pray it. I give her a parish bulletin with my phone number.

About a year later, the secretary of the parish gives me a note to call her, so I do, and she apologizes that it has been more than a year since we talked. "I even forgot your name, but my seven-year-old son remembered."

She asks me to pray for healing for people in her life. "Before we met you, my grandson had severe acid reflux, but after meeting you it has almost gone away. Could we meet to talk?"

"Most certainly!"

During our meeting she tells me she has been thinking of becoming Catholic. As I walk her to her car, she shows me the Rosary and Green Scapular hanging from the rear view mirror.

"I do not like to hang things from the mirror," she tells me, "but I thought these were so pretty. When people are driving recklessly, I hold the Rosary and scapular so they can see it and get a blessing to slow down."

"I hope you come to Mass to meet the nuns someday," I tell her.

I think it is essential to meet people where they are, to speak "heart to heart," to listen, and without compromising the truth, to lead them very slowly closer to God. People are on a journey, a pilgrimage. Some are practicing their love for God now, some are beginners, some are lost and worship the world, the flesh or the devil. From what I have seen, I think it takes a lot of courage to ask a priest to talk. Being on the streets breaks down barriers. "*Cor ad cor loquitor.*" "Heart speaks to heart." This element is essential to all missionary encounters.

We need to approach souls with delicacy and patience. Rating lifestyles on a moral scale of zero to ten (zero being assigned to satanism and ten to a life of prayer and good works like St. Mother Teresa's), when, for example, one meets someone at a level 3, the first impulse of zeal is to draw them up as quickly as possible, perhaps to a 7 on the first encounter. But I've realized that I can never do that. When someone is in a dark room and the lights are turned on too bright, it hurts their eyes and they shut them tight. When the soul is searching and is given too much light it can hurt so much that the soul may never return for more light. I have found it better to guide them from a 3 to a 3.1 or a 3.2 in the first encounter.

A woman having lunch with two others spots me through the window as I walk by a restaurant on the other side of the street. She comes outside and runs down the street to catch up with me, insisting I join her little luncheon. I can't resist her charity and enthusiasm, and inside, I offer a blessing over the food that is set before me.

"I have seen you walking everywhere, and I have always wanted to meet you," says the boisterous and joyful African American woman, who is well respected in the community. She wants to know where I am stationed so I show her a picture of the nuns and monastery on one of their CD's.

"I am a Baptist," Lauren says. "I think our pastor wants to meet you."

"Here is my card," I say. "I am a missionary priest. I bring people to the Holy Altars of God. Do you want to hear a story?"

"Yes," she says.

"In the seventeenth century, a man by the name of St. Francis de Sales would walk around the city of Chablais. He refused the horse or carriage because he wanted to be seen by the people. He would walk everywhere. Decades before his arrival, the city was all Catholic — 72,000 strong. After Calvin came, everyone became Calvinist except for 100 people. St. Francis de Sales was so gentle to people who wanted to meet him that word got around. They would experience his sweetness, witness his kind listening and hear his encouraging words. His motto was *cor ad cor loquitor*, heart speaks to heart."

I show her the coat of arms on the card of a bishop I know, whose motto is the same.

"The gold of St. Francis' heart and the sweetness of his words bore fruit among the people. He would write notes and slip them under people's doors. In three years, how many would you guess came back to the Catholic Faith?"

Lauren is unsure and guesses, "Half?"

"Zero!" I say. "His method was so gentle that it did not cause people to revert immediately. But even though there was little visible fruit, the seeds were being planted and were taking root. He continued this way, refusing to ride in a carriage. After twenty-five years, guess how many people were converted?"

Lauren just looks at me and shakes her head.

"Almost all 72,000 came back to the Catholic Faith!" I said.

Lauren wants me to meet her Protestant minister who is a fallen-away Catholic. She tells me she is going to connect me with him and two other men who do important work in the city. I pray that God rewards her for her kindness and beg for the grace to live a life of heroic prayer and virtue like St. Francis de Sales.

Francis' method will still work today because it comes from the example of our Lord himself. Jesus walked everywhere during his three years of public ministry.

While I was in the seminary, I had a spiritual director who said, "Jesus wants other people to walk the world as he walked the Holy Land." I have had these words burned in my mind ever since. I believe Jesus truly does call some of us to literally walk around as he did, going from town to town and country to country. The cassock is a profound help today because it is similar to the robe Jesus wore. I believe since it is a sacred garment, it attracts people of good will, people who are hungry for inspiration to lead a more God-like life. In all these stories, it was not so much what I said that inspired these people to give more to God, but rather, it was how I share the Faith with them—walking, praying and speaking with enthusiasm and happiness of my love for Jesus and His love for me. The experience of Jesus' love moves souls to great generosity.

"**T**oday it is very fashionable to talk about the poor. Unfortunately, it is not fashionable to talk *with* them.

St. Mother Teresa

9

In Search of Souls

Imagine walking by a beautiful monastery, with windows and doors open, the chanting of Solemn Vespers drifting out, incense billowing up to the ceiling, candle bearers standing by the abbot as he preaches the Gospel. Imagine how the soul, at this sight, would leave the ugly world behind and enter, as though through a gate of heaven, a Gothic Church, not in the stale atmosphere of a museum, but a church filled with dozens of canons regular in black robes, giving honor and glory in the Divine Offices day and night. In times past, it has been a particular charism of Canons Regular to offer a place for beautiful liturgies. If we receive this charism as described, people would come in and think, "I just entered the twelfth century, and I love it!" Beauty like this transcends time, and that is why these rich expressions of faith are just as relevant today as they were hundreds of years ago.

The Canons Regular I envision would follow the Rule of St. Augustine. The charism of the Canons Regular would fall between that of fully active parish priest and fully contemplative monks in a country monastery. The Canon Regular prays in the

97

morning with Gregorian Chant and says or attends two Masses in the city monastery. In the afternoon he would go out, like St. Martin, on the apostolate, to convert a culture steeped in darkness. The Canon Regular would come back for Vespers, a meal with table reading, recreation, Compline and monastic silence.

On most Thursdays, the nuns receive a food delivery and give me some food to take home. One day, they give me about twenty-five bananas. I put them in my book bag and begin walking. I stop an employee at a placement firm. Linda is the owner. I offer her and her employee Melissa some bananas. I walk a couple more blocks, and Tom honks his horn as he parks at T and G Rehab and Millwork. He is the owner of the small carpentry venture. I show him my Rosary and give him some bananas. I walk a couple of more blocks and see Stacey and her children on the front porch and give them some bananas. The kids eat them right away. I see Sherri at Hardee's, down about five more blocks, and I gave her my last two bananas. By the end of the day some people in town are talking about the priest who gives out bananas.

One day, I meet Timothy, a 24-year-old Protestant man and Nathan, 28, a Muslim. We chat about fifteen minutes, comparing religions. I ask them, "How would you like to see one of these abandoned churches converted into a monastery and some monks chanting the ancient Gregorian Chant? These canons regular could carry candles and incense and process around with a processional Crucifix." The two men are excited about the idea.

"My Muslim mentor once wanted to take me to a Catholic Mass," Nathan says.

We end our time together with me leading the "Lord's Prayer."

On another day, I am praying on the bench in the city square, and a young man walks up. I greet him with a smile. We talk for over thirty minutes about religion and his current journey to find a church. I find out that he is involved in the arts and music, and I offer him a compact disk of the nun's music: *Marian Hymns of Ephesus*, which he gladly took. I said, "Perhaps you would like to listen to the sisters live at a sung Mass some Sunday. They sing with natural organs, the windpipes of the human voice, which God created." I give him my card in case he has a desire to attend a Mass.

Some of these encounters are very brief. What I find so interesting is how many fallen-away Catholics are out there. So many of them want to come up and talk and share their spiritual problems so I can pray for them.

I meet "Linda" for a short talk. She promises she will start going back to Mass regularly after being away for decades. I meet "Joseph," an attorney, at the café. He is a fallen-away Catholic. A couple stops me by the side of a road to ask me what I do. One of them is a fallen-away Catholic. They both say that they love the cassock of a priest and the habits of the religious. A woman stops me in front of Starbucks and offers me food. She left the Catholic Church five years ago and works for the Salvation Army. I meet "Sandra" who is taking groceries to her house from her van parked on the street. She calls her husband, a truck-driver, as she was driving home and told him she saw me crossing the rail road tracks. She tells me that she fell away from the Church after so much changed in the 1960's, after Vatican II. A 25-year-old man I meet tells me he is a fallen-away Catholic and then asks for prayers for health and financial problems.

A young man and his father approach me as I am walking along the sidewalk in downtown St. Joseph. They ask what I am doing. I tell them, "I am a missionary priest. I walk around town praying the Rosary and carrying this Crucifix. I am trying to unite myself with God by meditating on the mysteries of His life, death and resurrection."

They are both encouraging. "You are so generous to come from Kansas simply to walk the streets to bring people the Light of Jesus!"

We talk some more, and I affirm the young man in his decision to join the military.

A few months later, I am walking in the park downtown by St. Joseph City Hall. I am resting on the steps when that father comes over to tell me some good news about his son.

"He told me after meeting you and seeing your efforts to come to the people in the streets, 'Dad, I was so encouraged by meeting Father Carney that I want to do something for God. Instead of joining the military service of the Marines, I want to join the religious ministry and become a chaplain.' Father Carney, I cannot tell you what a positive impact you made on my son and me! We think it is the most God-inspiring thing ever to walk the streets."

I am drinking tea and studying Latin outside the tattoo parlor when the owner and two of his friends approach. One of the men, whom I will call Anthony, must have heard about me.

"Do you have any sacred medals to hand out?" he asks.

"Of course."

Each picks out a medal as I have them in a mound in my hand. Anthony picks the Miraculous Medal. I explain, "The Blessed Virgin Mary, the Mother of God is stamped on that medal. It is called the Miraculous Medal. If you say this prayer you will be blessed, 'Oh Mary, conceived without sin, pray for us, who have recourse to thee.' If you wear this medal every day and say that prayer for a month, God will bless you."

It is a month later now and I see Anthony, his mother and

his girlfriend as we were all entering a store.

His mom says, "Father, I have wanted to meet you. You have done so much for my son." I thanked her for the kind words.

While waiting in line to check out, Anthony and I have a private conversation. He says, "Father, I have gotten into some trouble. But I want to be an upstanding, honest man. I want to marry my girlfriend."

"You have chosen well," I tell him. "The wise man is virtuous and delights in the laws of God. Society teaches men to give in to sin. But the word *virtus* is Latin and has the root *vir*, which means *man*. An honest man puts aside temptation and practices virtue. Virtue is manly. Your girlfriend has a natural built-in attraction to men of virtue. Now is one of the most important times in your life. You can decide to practice bad habits, giving into temptation from the devil, or to stand guard for your soul, your future wife and your future children. You are the man in your future family. God has designed the man as the spiritual leader of the family. I know you do not go to church right now, but that is a step that you need to take, and I have just the thing to help you make the best decisions in your life. The Mother of God, the Blessed Virgin Mary, will communicate to you the power of God if you ask her for the Divine Fire of God to defend you from the enemy of your soul. The second greatest weapon from evil is the Rosary. I am going to give each of you one, if you want."

Anthony listens carefully to each word. He picks up the Miraculous Medal that he is wearing. "Father, I have prayed that prayer since you gave me this medal a month ago. It has really helped me."

I give Anthony, his mom and his girlfriend a Rosary and the pamphlet on "How to pray the Rosary" produced by the nuns.

Imagine these Divine Meetings happening regularly. If fifty men who loved the Church and want to save souls were given to the streets in the city of St. Joseph, or wherever God wants this to happen, how long would it take for the city to convert? Once again, St. Francis de Sales had no converts in his first three years. But after twenty-five years, walking the streets and giving instruction with the gentleness of the Holy Spirit, he brought 72,000 back to the Catholic Faith. The Center for Applied Research in the Apostolate estimates that 25 Million Catholics have fallen away from the church in the United States. That is about 25% of baptized Catholics. "And my sheep were scattered, because there was no shepherd: and they became the prey of all the beasts of the field, and were scattered. My sheep wandered in every mountain, and in every high hill: and my flocks were scattered upon the face of the earth, and there was none that sought them, there was none, I say, that sought them."[1]

I am walking one day in Hazel Park, Michigan, when I see about a dozen teenagers playing in a park. After I pray for them, one of the kids stops me and asks about the Rosary. Since it is October, I speak to them about All Hallow's Eve. "All Hallows Eve celebrates all the Saints in Heaven on November first and all the Souls that are waiting in Purgatory on November second. Purgatory that place where a soul 'pays for its sins.' It is like this, for example: a kid accidentally hits a baseball through his neighbor's window. If he is a good boy, he goes over, knocks on the door and tells Mabel, 'I am sorry I broke your window.' Mabel responds, 'Johnny, I accept your apology, but I am on a limited income. I need you to pay for it.' So Johnny, being a good boy, starts a little business, lawn mowing or running a Kool-aid stand, makes the hundred dollars and gives it to Mabel for the window."

"You see kids, we commit sin before God our Father

---

1   Ezekiel xxxiv: 5-6

and ask for forgiveness. He always forgives a contrite heart, but sometimes we have to pay a debt for our sins. Purgatory is a place where we pay that remaining debt of punishment for our sin. Johnny asked for forgiveness, Mabel gave forgiveness, but the debt of restoring the window was Johnny's responsibility. In other words, God holds us responsible to pay the debt of punishment due for our sins. Jesus is our Redeemer, His blood restores the relationship between God and sinner. It takes an infinite offering to restore a relationship with the infinite God. Jesus does that for us. But, in the order of justice, God still requires the sinner to pay the debt for sin. The Church encourages us to pay the debt for our sins during this life by voluntary penance and good works. But if any debt remains when we die, we must suffer the payment of it before entering heaven."

"We can help to pay the punishment of sin for those who wait in Purgatory. In the analogy, Johnny could have received help to pay the one hundred dollars. God allows us to pray for the dead so they will get to heaven faster.

The Church devotes one day each year to the joyous celebration of all the saints, who attained heaven by God's help and are now eager to help us in our spiritual battles. They want us to escape the fires of hell and even purgatory by a life of heroic virtue, so that death will bring us straight to the joys of heaven. Since it is such a prominent celebration, the festivities of All Saints Day begin the evening preceding, on All Hallows Eve (or in Old English, Halloween), 'Hallows' referring the holiness of the saints and the blessed ground where they are buried. It is followed by the observance of All Souls Day, a day of penance and supplication on behalf of the poor suffering souls in purgatory. The devil, the enemy of our happiness, wants to distract us from these grace-filed liturgical observances and all the good we can do for souls. He tries to usurp them for his own purposes, so that Halloween has become an occasion for wearing grotesque costumes which celebrate evil rather then the lives of great saints like St. Patrick.

I walk past a Taco Bell, smile and wave at a lady. She stops me and asks, "Now fellow, what are you about?"

"I am a missionary priest."

"Are you for real?"

I explain to her why I wear the cassock and pray the Rosary. Before leaving, we exchange contact info. Her name is Sherri.

I follow up in a text: "Do you like line art?"

"What is line art?" she asks.

"Line art uses wood carvings to print black and white pictures. It is found in old Roman Missals. My favorite Catechism is *A Manual of Religion: My Catholic Faith: A Catechism in Pictures.* I like it for two reasons: first, it was written by a bishop; and second, it has very beautiful and detailed pictures that explain the faith in art." People who did not grow up Catholic often receive the Faith more effectively by sacred art than theological questions and answers.

Sherri and I agree to meet at Hardees.

I bring the Catechism and show her the line art that depicts the importance of remaining pure. During the lesson, she requests to come to Mass on Sunday.

Periodically, Sherri and I meet at Hardees to read over a chapter in the Cathechism. Often people are curious, and they come to our table to see what we were doing. One man, named Travis, asks if priests are married. I explain how in the Latin Rite it is extremely rare. Another man asks what I called my outfit. I tell him it is a cassock and answer some of his other questions

Another day, I meet with Sherri at Cafè Pony Espresso

and four others join us. One of the group, a woman named Lynn, sees my fourteen-inch Crucifix and asks, "Why is Jesus on there?" I also meet the other three: Jason, Amber and Elia.

A few days later some of these people find me at Hardees. I buy them cheeseburgers. During our conversation, Joshua tells me pictures fly off his wall since he played with an ouija board. I give him some Epiphany Water to sprinkle. (Epiphany water is blessed once a year on the evening before the feast of Epiphany. It starts with the Litany of Saints, then continues with the chanting of Psalms 28, 45, and 146, commenting on the glory, honor, refuge, help, and joy we experience in the presence of Our God. There is then a prayer of exorcism against Satan and the apostate angels. Then the Canticle of Zachary or the Canticle of the Blessed Virgin Mary are chanted. These are followed by a prayer addressed to God speaking of the revelation of the Faith to the Gentiles. An exorcism of salt is next, followed by a blessing for the all powerful clemency of God. An exorcism of water is said, followed by the blessing of water, recalling the salvation of mankind through water. The rite continues with the mixing of the salt and water with the Sign of the Cross three times. Another prayer, asking for the power of God the King to give us triumph over our enemies, is said and followed with the chant called the *Te Deum*. It takes about forty-five minutes.)

I show Joshua how to make the sign of the cross to ask for protection from evil.

I explain that the Sign of the Cross is not magic or superstition, but a sacramental of the Church. There are important differences between magic and prayers. Magic addresses itself to the enemies of God in the preternatural world, or angelic world. In other words, a spell, curse, hex, etc. addresses fallen angels, also known as demons. Magic seeks to exercise power beyond ordinary human nature — a power thus termed preternatural — through the instrumentality of these demonic beings. Although demons relinquished a great deal of their natural power when they fell from grace, God still allows them to exercise it to some extent.

Unlike magic, the prayer of the Church Militant (Christians on earth) addresses itself to God, either directly, or through intercessory meditation of His friends, the Church Triumphant (angels and saints in heaven) and the Church Suffering (souls in purgatory). And, whereas magic expresses itself in pride, as a demand, prayer takes the form of humble supplication, asking rather than demanding.

While I give instructions on another day, a lady comes up and tells me she hasn't been to Mass for decades. She promises me that she will start going back to the Holy Sacrifice of the Mass regularly. Two other people approach and ask me some questions. One admits he had signed up for the Rite of Christian Initiation of Adults, but dropped out. The other asked to be baptized. Another man asks me about angels. After that discussion, he goes off on a tangent about his belief in evolution. I go back to giving instructions, then he leaves, but I give him a bulletin with my phone number. He calls that evening.

He says, "Father, I apologize for the way I acted."

"I appreciate your apology," I say. "I enjoy having conversations, which means, 'to be with (con) the truth (ver).' We savor the truth. Evolution is still just an unproven theory, so we must not treat it like a physical law, but rather as a theory that could very well be proved wrong some day. At the end of the day I want to approach the truth, because Jesus said, 'The truth will set you free.'"

Another day of instructions at Hardee's gives me the opportunity to meet a truck driver, who tells me "I have heard about you," and a fallen-away Catholic who comes up to shake my hand and wants to look at my Crucifix and Rosary. After a ten minute conversation, he leaves with a parish bulletin that I have given him. I sometimes carry old parish bulletins with me and hand them out, with a personal note and my contact.

Another day, I meet Beatrice, an assistant minister at a Protestant church. She requests prayers from the nuns for the intention, "union with the Most Holy Trinity." She tells me her favorite verse of the Bible. It is from Isaiah. "Here I am Lord, I come to do your will." I tell her my favorite verse, "He who eateth my flesh, and drinketh my blood, abideth in me, and I in him."[2] Another person asks, "How are you doing?" I reply, "better than ever!" When he leaves, my student, whom I had met there to give lessons on the Catechism, says, "He was the former Mayor of St. Joseph."

Another lady, Amber, comes up and asks, "Can you pray for me that God directs my path?"

I receive a call from Alison, "Father, I heard about you from the Brown family. I see you walking on Fourth Street and want to meet you, but I have to pick up my child from basketball. I told him, 'Look for the priest. He is wearing a hat that looks like St. Damian's.'" She invited me to dinner with the Brown family. The Browns were among the first people I met in St. Joseph on the Rosary Walk.

One day in the Stockyards, two ladies call me from their car asking if they can take my picture. I am on the sidewalk and quite a distance from the road because a large ditch separates us, so I yell back, "Yes, you may take my picture." They snap a photo, and one of the ladies says she wants to talk some day and that she really appreciates my work.

About six months later, a lady comes running after me just as I cross the street. "Do you remember me?" she asks.

I tell her I don't.

"I saw you in the stockyards and asked to take your picture and you said, 'yes.'"

I paused to think. "Oh yes, I remember."

"I am an addict. I felt ever since I met you that I was not doing right until I got to talk to you. I saw another priest from behind and thought it might be you, but when I spoke to him

_____

2   Jn. vi:57

I found out it was not you. I asked about you and he told me how to find you. But I told him that I would just wait and see if I run into you again, so here we are. Do you have time to talk?"

"Yes, I have some time right now."

She tells me her problems: addiction, divorce, remarriage and another impending divorce, jail terms.

She continues, "While in prison, I had time to reflect. Although my mother was Catholic and my father was Baptist, I never got baptized. I always knew that I should, so I got baptized, and it started to change me."

I encourage her: "Do you know what happened when you were baptized? A valid baptism puts the Passion of Jesus in your soul." I picked up the Crucifix. "His suffering was offered to His Father, and His offering was accepted. We who are baptized receive the reward of His perfect offering. Once baptized, a soul has the ability to receive Sanctifying Grace. Sanctifying Grace is the life that God puts into souls who are in the state of Grace. Did you know that an angel appeared to the Mother of Jesus and said, "Hail full of grace..." If she is full of grace, is she lacking grace?"

She says, "No."

I continue, "She was full of God. The angel said, 'The Lord is with you.' Did you know that she went to see Elizabeth? Upon greeting Mary, Elizabeth said to her, 'Blessed art thou amongst women.' We all know about Mary, the Mother of God! Do you know that your soul too can be filled with grace?"

She pauses and says finally, "Yes, that makes sense."

"Do you think having the life of God in us makes us happy?"

"Yes, I love having moments of happiness."

"There are thrones in heaven open for us to take because about one third of the angels revolted and fell from grace. These could also be explained as mansions. The closer the dwelling is to God, the bigger and more glorious it is. The edge of heaven is for the souls who barely made it. They dwell in small homes in comparison. The amount that we love God, neighbor and our self for the sake of God determines our reward, our glory in heaven. We can start living heaven here on earth. You mentioned that you liked moments of happiness. How would you like hours of happiness every day?"

She is astonished, "You are happy for hours?"

I tell her what Jesus promised: "Amen, I say to you, there is no one who has given up house or brothers or sisters or mother or father or children or lands for my sake and for the sake of the Gospel who will not receive a hundred times more now in this present age … and eternal life in the age to come."[3]

Then I ask her, "Did you know that priests have left everything? We do not get married. We are practicing for heaven now. We are here to encourage others who struggle with intemperance by giving up a good, marriage, for a greater good, to imitate Jesus who never married. I am happy for hours. Do you want to know why?"

She starts to cry, "I never knew you priests did not get married. Yes, tell me."

"We were made to be in union with God. After baptism, we can be filled with Sanctifying Grace. This is a gift that God generously gives to those who turn away from sin and ask for grace. The Blessed Virgin Mary is the best example of this. She was 'full of grace.' God literally dwelt in her womb. 'The Lord is with thee.' We who turn away from sin and ask God for a pure heart, a good heart like you have, (she began to cry as I continued), are disposed to receive Him. When we are filled with God, we are happy." I show her my Rosary, "This Rosary helps me to think and reflect upon the mystery of Mary being filled with God. When I think of God all day long, it makes me very happy. Now the devil does not want us to be happy. He wants to take us to hell so we will be subject to him. That is why he tempts us with intemperance, through empty pleasures like drugs or fornication. These may give us

---

3   Mark 10:29-30

moments of happiness, but they are a trick."

She responds, "Yes, drugs do not make me happy. They only numb me for a few moments, but overall, they have made me sad. Can I have a Rosary?"

I ask her what color she likes, and she picks out a Rosary and takes a pamphlet on how to pray the Rosary. I teach her how to make the Sign of the Cross and pray the Apostles Creed, the Our Father and the Hail Mary. After an hour I say my good-byes. She says, "Father, thanks for your card, I will keep in touch."

One day, a walking companion and I pass by the jail, and a woman in her early seventies gets out of her parked car in front of the jail. Leaving a young lady sitting in the passenger's side, she smiles and comes up to me.

"Father, my name is Barbara. I have always wanted to meet you. You have helped my granddaughter and my great grandchildren down in the south of town. They showed me the medals you gave them. I was wondering if you could bless my Miraculous Medal and give a medal to my great granddaughter who is incarcerated?"

She put out her hand and I shake it and say, "Barbara, you have made my day. Let me ask, are those great grandchildren of yours living on Tenth Street?"

She answers, "Yes, they were until they moved."

I ask where they moved and she tells me they have relocated out into the country.

She continues, "Father, I just love what you are doing. I am a convert. The happiest days of my life were at Sacred Heart High School." The school was started in the first half of the nineteenth century by the influence of St. Rose Philippine Duchesne. It was closed and demolished in the 1960's.

Barbara continues, "I almost became a nun. The nuns were very special to me and the other students."

The young girl gets out of the car and comes over to us.

"I want you to meet my granddaughter," Barbara said. "I take her for counseling. She has just gotten with the wrong crowd."

"Hi, I am Fr. Carney," I say. "Would you like to see a picture of some nuns? It is so peaceful here." I take out the CD made by the Benedictines of Mary, Queen of Apostles, and show her the pictures of the singing nuns. "It may be good for you to make a visit, come to Mass and ask the nuns to pray for you to find your way."

She says, "Yes, maybe I could do that, but first I have to get out of jail. I have to go now. They want me back."

Barbara says good-bye to her granddaughter then asks me, "Father, do you have a medal of St. Christopher?"

"I doubt it, but let me look."

I search through the medals a friend has collected from people who no longer want them. I believe there were over two hundred, but now the collection has shrunk to around a hundred. It is toward the end of the search, when, to my surprise, I find a medal of St. Christopher!

I exclaim, "I cannot believe it, I did not think I had one, but here is a medal of St. Christopher!" I give her the medal and we exchange contact information and speak about a possible visit to the nuns and the possibility of Barbara joining me on the Rosary walk.

Sometimes, I meet people who drink too much and say things that are a little alarming. One day I meet a man in his late fifties who is a bit drunk. He says, "What are you doing? Don't be walking around here with that Crucifix. You will get hurt. There are people around here who won't like you."

As he continues, I think, "This guy is full of it. I have never had problems in the last year with anybody."

He continues, "Get out of here while you still can." He curses a little and then says, "I do not mean to curse."

"Well, I must be going," I say, and we go our separate ways.

About three or four months later, he calls me over to his porch saying similar things to scare me, but then he offers his hand and I give his hand a shake. He looks me in the eye for the first time. Then I say, "Well, I need to keep moving along."

About six weeks later, he calls me over to his porch again. "You are nice," he says. "I like you. Would you like a cigarette?"

I gracefully decline.

"Why do you like God?" he asks. "I cannot believe God would take my five year old child. He is not a good God. Why did He do that? I drink to forget about it." I notice that his features – the deep lines in his face, the leathery skin – reveal years of alcohol abuse. He continues sharing his memories of losing his child. A young lady comes from behind the house and asks about the Rosary hanging from my wrist. I ask her if she wants one. The man says, "Yes, that would be good to get a Rosary from him. He is nice."

I take out the Rosaries and the pamphlets.

She picks one and then asks, "Can I have another for my friend?"

"Of course," I say. "Here is how to pray the *Hail Mary*."

After we finish the prayer, I give them my priestly blessing and continue on my way. I wonder if I will get to meet him again.

"We were made to be in union with God...When we are filled with God, we are happy."

Photo by Bob Travaglione

"Today, as in the past, it is the saints who are the most effective evangelizers, and all the baptized are called to aspire to this high standard of ordinary Christian living.

St. John Paul II

10

Upon This Rock

I am always aware that I am sowing seeds, in hopes that someday there will be a harvest. God sends me to whom He wishes to reach.

Today, I am walking and praying with a seminarian. We pass by a man named Hermon, who in his usual friendly manner, smiles at us and says, "Father, is this another priest in training?"

"Yes, this is Michael, a seminarian."

Hermon introduces me to another man standing next to his truck with a mower in the bed.

"Father, I used to go to the Cathedral," the man says, "but it has been years."

I tell him, "There is a very friendly priest there. You ought to go and talk to him."

I give him my card.

"Father," he says, "I do not know the Faith."

"If you stay in touch, I will make sure that you get the help you need."

If he stays in touch, I will become his spiritual coach and

encourage him to come to God by the most expedient means. This could mean that I give him private instructions on the Catechism, Sacraments, Prayer and the Bible. Or I could have him meet with the local pastor who would provide all that is necessary to live the Catholic faith.

On one of my walks, I meet a fallen-away Jewish woman. She likes my zucchetto, a scull cap worn by Catholic clergy. It is similar to the yarmulke that Jewish men wear during sacred ceremonies. I take my zucchetto off to show her the Sacred Heart badge sewn on the inside.

I teach her the prayer I say when I kiss the Sacred Heart: "O Jesus, meek and humble of heart, make my heart more like unto Thine." She shows me a picture of Jesus she carries with her. We have a long talk about God. I ask, "Is it all right if the nuns pray for you?"

She is happy about that question. I show her the CDs of the nuns' music. She writes down twenty-one names of people in her family in need of the nuns' prayers.

I am walking from my brother's house in Kansas City to Old St. Patrick's Church to say Mass. Along the way I see a young man in his mid-twenties listening to music. I say a prayer for him. Two blocks later, he catches up with me.

His name is Augustine, and he is a college student and an atheist. He tells me the name of the college and I say, "I know a young man there named Austin. Do you know him?"

He did! We have an hour-long conversation about why he left the Catholic Church and became an atheist. We take a slight detour, and I bring him to the "Catholic Center," the chancery for the Kansas City–St. Joseph Diocese. It has a beautiful chapel. We go in to pray. As we leave, he expresses his joy in our conversation.

"Do you have Austin's phone number?" I ask.

"Yes. Do you want me to call him?"

"Certainly."

Augustine dials the number and hands me the phone. I tell Austin I am just calling to say hello because I just met a mutual classmate. We finish our chat, and I say good bye and continue to Old St. Patrick's church to say Mass. This is a conversation that could not have happened if I had driven to Mass. I walk these streets to help people know God, and that's an important aspect of my ministry, but I am also very aware that encounters like this depend on another source of grace for their efficacy.

The whole world unknowingly revolves around the Holy Sacrifice of the Mass. Every Mass extends the Kingdom of God, and a priest is encouraged to say Mass every day. We will not know the value of each Mass until entering eternity. One time, I went into a church and found a priest in the back praying while a Mass was being offered at the altar. I knew this priest had already offered Mass that day, so I later asked him why he was present at that second Mass. He explained that he regularly prayed in the presence of a second Holy Mass as part of his daily holy hour. "Jesus is there on Calvary, so you can offer Him your petitions, because the priest is in the person of Christ," he said. Since then, I have taken the advice and attend a second Mass and pray there quietly.

I sometimes encourage the faithful at Mass, "What happens in here determines what happens out there." This is because the Holy Mass is a re-presentation of the sacrifice of Jesus the High Priest to His Father on the cross. At Holy Mass, we enter into this sacrifice, and the more authentically we pray with pure intentions joined to Our Lord's perfect offering to the Father, the more graces are won for the world. This is why reverence is so important and helpful. The outward gestures of reverence—kneeling, silence, bows, etc.—help us to recognize and recall the spiritual reality taking place on the altar.

On my ordination day on May 26, 2007, I received what I had been desiring for so long: a real participation in the priestly love of Jesus. When Jesus left the earth, He promised to remain with His people, and so He sent us the Holy Spirit and established the Church. Now Jesus wants to give Himself and His salvation to the world through the workings of the Holy Spirit carrying out His plan by means of the Church. As representatives of the Church, priests are anointed as mediators between God and God's children, thus we are called "Father." When I offer Holy Mass, I feel like there is a great spiritual power to do good. I am often reminded of Moses holding up his hands in the battle against the enemies of Israel. In the silence of the Mass, when I am holding my hands up, I think of the power of God stopping the evil in the world. I also think of all the people who have asked me to pray for them, and I am standing as a mediator between them and God as if I am a bridge between heaven and earth. Then it's a profound mystery when I think about receiving Almighty God in Holy Communion and all the good that can be done by allowing His power to move me. Jesus borrows my whole being! I become like Him in a mysterious way when I speak the words of consecration at Mass and absolution in Confession. I feed my spiritual children in body and soul with the Bread of Life. It also means I get to be a father to the people on the streets.

One day, I decide to take a tea break at a gas station I have never visited. A young man in his early twenties lets me get free hot water and ice, so I can brew my tea. We start chatting, and he tells me his dad is the owner of the gas station. He also tells me that he is a fallen away member of the Catholic Church.

"Are you going to become a saint?" I ask him. And then I clarify, "A canonized saint?"

A customer comes in, so I leave, but I return several times after that. The gas station owner's son is always too busy to get into any kind of meaningful conversation, but I hope he remembers my question. It has been almost a year. I hope to have time some day to pick up where we left off.

I am out walking when five high school kids pull up beside me and ask for gas money. I tell them I will meet them at the gas station in ten minutes. When they pull up, I ask them, "How much gas do you want me to buy?"

"Oh, three dollars," the driver says.

After I pay, I see a Rosary hanging from the neck of one of the passengers.

"Where did you get that Rosary?" I ask.

"I got it online."

"I have free Rosaries in my book bag, and since I am a priest, I can bless them right here. Who wants one?"

They all do.

I talk to them about God for about ten minutes, bless the Rosaries and give them each one. I give them an old bulletin and write down my phone number.

They never do call me back, nor have I seen them again. From what I have seen, people are very shy about calling a priest because they say that priests are "too busy."

That is why I walk. Picking up where you left off happens quite often and naturally when we walk the streets. It is easy for a person to have a conversation with a priest when he is traveling the sidewalk. I am not "too busy." I am available.

I walk by an artist standing out in front of his studio in New Orleans.

"What are you doing?" he asks.

"I am walking and praying."

He asks me to bless his St. Benedict medal and his studio.

Another mile down the street, I see a beautiful statue of Mary in someone's front yard. I pray for a moment, and then the woman who lives there comes out and asks me to bless her house. She says she used to go to the nuns' Mass. I invite her to resume daily attendance at Mass. I say, "According to a pious saying, attending one Mass with devotion raises the glory of the soul one degree in heaven for eternity!"

About half a mile later, I find a park bench next to the bayou. A man named Chip comes up to talk. He ran a meal kitchen for the poor in New Orleans until the law required him to stop. We chat about God for awhile. As I leave the park, I run into two young mothers with their children. After introductions, one of the women tells me she is a fallen-away Catholic. The other is a practicing Catholic. In our fifteen minute conversation, I tell the former why she should go back to the Catholic Church.

"You should receive the Body of Jesus Christ," I say.

Both women are so thankful for our providential meeting.

The next day, I walk by the park again. It is full of people of all ages. A group of boys between the ages of nine and fourteen come up to me, asking about my cassock.

"What do you think these five buttons on my sleeve mean?" I ask them. "Do you need a hint?"

I point at my left hand, then my right, my left foot, then the right and my side as I count, "One, two, three, four, five."

One of the boys raises his hand. "The five wounds!" he exclaims.

"Congratulations! See boys, you know more than you think. Now, how old was Jesus when he died? Hint: the answer is on my cassock."

They are stumped.

"My cassock has thirty-three buttons. Theologians believe Jesus was thirty-three when He was crucified."

I say goodbye and continue on my way. A few minutes later, I look back and see them jumping off the dock into the bayou. I had a little chuckle as I contemplated the carefree days of youth.

In south Louisiana, the people are very Catholic. I especially like their custom of painting their outdoor statues of the Blessed Virgin Mary pastel colors. One day, I stop in front of a house to look at a very beautiful statue of Mary and say a prayer. The people who live there see me and the father invites me in. He introduces me to his wife and daughter. He offers me some Italian food and asks me to bless the house. After the blessing, we get into a discussion about religion.

He says, "I do not believe it matters which church you belong to as long as you believe in God."

"Allow me and the nuns to pray for you," I say. He gives his permission and I invite him to Mass before I leave.

It is very difficult to know when to argue and when to listen. It does matter which church one belongs to. There is only one Church founded by God. The Catholic Church was founded by Jesus Christ Himself, when he told Peter, the first Pope, "Upon this rock, I build my Church." Every other church was founded by a creature. It is only through Jesus Christ that we are saved. I could have told that man all of this. But sometimes prudence requires me to hold off until people start asking questions. It is important to win the city over by charity first, then to win them over to the Catholic Church. Every encounter is different. A life of deep prayer helps me to know when to speak and when to listen.

That same day a young lady comes up to me asking for prayers. She has been in jail for drugs, so I speak about the devil and his influence. I pray some prayers over her then invite her to Holy Thursday Mass. Soon after that another young lady wants to be prayed over. She tells me she keeps landing in jail. After I pray, I give her a prayer card of "Our Lady of Remedy."

Back in St. Joseph, a friend of mine, Eric, has decided to join me on some walks in St. Joseph, offering the Rosary for the intention of the conversion of the souls we meet. We see a man with his five boys down the street. They motion for us to come over. The father tells me he has spent some time in jail, but he reads the Bible.

"I want to help my boys to be good," he says. "But one time, I needed some support from a church, but they told me, 'Only if you are a member.'"

"The Catholic Church helps those in need even if they are not members," I tell him. "And the word 'Catholic' means universal. Everyone can become a member of the Catholic Church. Shall we gather your boys and say a prayer?"

The man, whose name is Michael, calls all the boys and I hand them each a holy card of "Mary, Queen of our Hearts."

One of the boys must think this is a different kind of card because he asks if we can play a game.

"Oh yes, I almost forgot," I say. "Who knows how to make the sign of the cross?"

No one knows. I demonstrate a few times, then I say, "Now each of you try it on your own."

After each boy "passes," I give them a card, pray the prayer, and we part ways.

I think to myself, "That is why I desire to walk. There are so many drug abusers who want out of that horrible life. We can walk around town, find them and help them change their lives."

St. Alphonsus de Liguori, in *The True Spouse of Jesus Christ,* relates how the greatest sinners can become the most eminent saints.

"Such lives as St. Mary Magdalene, St. Augustine, St. Pelagia, St. Mary of Egypt, and especially of St. Margaret of Cortona, who was for many years in the state of damnation, but even then cherished a desire of sanctity; and who after her conversion, flew to perfection with such rapidity, that she merited to learn by revelation even in this life, not only that she was predestined to glory, but also that a place was prepared for her among the seraphim."[1]

---

1   St. Alphonsus de Liguori, *The True Spouse of Jesus Christ*, Redemptorists Fathers, 1929, p. 87

I walk past the front yard of a sixty-year-old grandmother of four teenagers. She calls after me and asks me to come back. She first asks about the cassock, then the saturno and the Crucifix. We talk for about an hour, and she keeps repeating, throughout the conversation, how much she likes the cassock. Two of the boys ask me to play basketball, but I accept Shirley's offer of soup and crackers. As the soup simmers, I get to visit with her. I encourage her to read the Bible, so she goes into the house and brings out the Bible and reads the first two paragraphs of Ruth. She says her family is Pentecostal now, but she takes out her grandmother's Rosary and shows it to me. I give her a pamphlet "How to pray the Rosary."

I think she wants to talk to me because I was praying a Rosary and wearing a cassock. Both are sacramentals that have a spiritual draw. They are also beautiful and inspire wonder in the observer. Although she is Pentecostal, she is interested in hearing about the ancient faith of her grandmother, Catholicism. I imagine, as is the case with many people I meet, that the Faith of her ancestors was not passed on to her properly. But God gives her a chance, at this particular moment, to be introduced to that Faith, since a priest is walking by her house.

I sit at a table on the sidewalk outside downtown St. Joseph, drinking my tea. Kevin, whom I met at the local soup kitchen, walks up. I greet him and offer him something from the tea shop with my gift certificate. He returns with yogurt, when at the same moment a lady leaving the health store next door says to the clerk, "Thanks for getting me the yogurt." I turn to her and say, "How ironic that I hear you speaking about yogurt when Kevin got himself some yogurt."

She responds, "What are you doing over here?" I tell her that I just meet people walking by and talk about God. I have a holy card of the Litany of the Immaculate Heart of Mary, my

Rosary, and my Crucifix lying on the table. She asks, "What kind of an order do you belong to?" The answer leads us into an hour-long conversation. It becomes a question and answer session about the different beliefs of the Catholic faith and Protestantism.

We cover the sacraments of Baptism, the Holy Sacrament of the Altar, Penance, and Holy Orders. My favorite part of the discussion was explaining the Catholic view that the Bible is not the sole source of Revelation.

She says, "It is only by following the written Word of God that we can be saved."

"What about a person who died in the year forty AD?" I say. "That was before the first New Testament book was written. Are you saying that since the Bible was not yet written, that person could not be saved?"

She responds, "Well there are types in the Old Covenant, foreshadowing what was to come in the New Testament."

"OK yes," I agree. "What you say is true. But when Jesus instituted the New Covenant, around thirty-three AD, was the Old Covenant superceded?"

"That is a good point," she says.

I continue explaining how the Old Covenant sacrifice lost its efficacy at the time they killed Jesus.

At the end, she explains her concern that I honor the Blessed Virgin Mary too much. She reads to me one of her favorite passages in the Bible from Hebrews, "Now of the things which we have spoken, this is the sum: We have such a high priest, who is set on the right hand of the throne of the majesty in the heavens."[2] She continues, "It does not say that Mary is at the right hand of the throne, it is only Jesus the high priest."

After she points out a number of "problems" with focusing "too much" on Mary, I say, "Madame, please do not denigrate the Blessed Virgin Mary!" Earlier in our conversation

---

2   Hebrews viii: 1

I had already explained that we give adoration to God alone but we give veneration to all the saints, and among the saints, we give the highest honor to the Blessed Virgin Mary and to St. Joseph because of their role in salvation history.

"Jesus wants us to love Mary more. Mary wants us to love Jesus more. Does not a good son want his mother to be honored?"

She pauses and reflects. Then after cordial remarks, we go our way. I question myself. Was I too firm? Was I not firm enough? I hope I will see her again, and we can continue our conversation.

"Tony" thinks he is going to hell. The 75-year-old man is a fallen-away Catholic. The last time he went to church was 1965. He wants to talk about forgiveness.

I met with him first in May of 2014.

It's August now of the following year when I walk into the soup kitchen and see him there.

He asks me to sit with him during lunch. I sit down and begin my soup kitchen protocol: put out the Rosaries, the sacred metals, some prayer cards and my Crucifix on the table in front of me.

"Father I am so glad that I get to see you again," Tony says. "I have been wanting to talk to you some more about forgiveness." During a previous meeting, he told me he had spent time in jail and was kicked out of a few Protestant churches. He again shares with me his grave concern that he is going to Hell. During our conversation, I am interrupted four times, by people drawn to the holy items lying on the table. I hand out rosaries, explain how to pray, give out a couple of Miraculous Medals. A lady picks up a card called, "Mary, Queen of our Hearts." It has a picture of the Blessed Virgin Mary, wearing a crown, holding the Child Jesus as Jesus holds the world in his arms. At the same time, she is giving a heart with a fire on top of it to St. Louis de Montfort. The other side has a beautiful prayer called, "Efficacious Prayer to Mary, Queen of our Hearts."

I return to my conversation with Tony. I tell him how to prepare for the sacrament of Confession. I tell him that this is the first step necessary to continue his full practice of the faith. His friend is leaving so he needs to go, but I can tell he wants to continue our conversation. When he leaves, I think: "He last went to the Holy Sacrifice of the Mass in 1965. If he resumes Mass attendance that will be a fifty-year gap." I begin to pray the Rosary for Tony. After about a decade or two, a middle-aged woman named Laura sits down next to me to have her lunch. After some small talk it is time to go, so I put all the sacramentals in my backpack and continue my Rosary Walk, praying for Tony to come back home.

"From what I have seen, people are very shy about calling a priest because they say that priests are 'too busy.' That is why I walk ... It is easy for a person to have a conversation with a priest when he is traveling the sidewalk. I am not 'too busy.' I am available."

Photo by Jeanne Meyer

"In meditation we find the strength to bring Christ to birth in ourselves and in other men.

St. Charles Borromeo

11

Down by the Bayou

I arrive in New Orleans in the late summer of 2015. My host asks, "Father, what do you want to do?"

"I want to walk around the block," I answer.

As I am walking, I have a thought: "Go to a nearby church and pray before the Blessed Sacrament."

The church is about six blocks away. When I arrive, I try to get in but every entrance is locked. I walk through the parish campus, then turn around and start to go back the way I came. But then I think, "Walking around the block does not mean walking back the way you came. It means going to the other street to make your way back by a different route." So I walk to the other side of the parish. I see moss growing from a tree, and go closer to feel it. I only see this kind of moss when I travel to south Louisiana. It hangs from the tree branches, sometimes over a foot long. I am curious to touch it since it does not grow in my native Kansas. As I walk to the tree, I glance inside a window and see a group of ladies meeting in a building next to the parking lot. I touch the moss and I gaze at the bayou. Storm clouds partially cover the evening sun, setting the sky ablaze. I am lost in thought, contemplating the power and beauty of God.

"Father, are you lost?"

A woman had come out from the building.

"No," I say, "I am just walking around the block."

"We are having a Legion of Mary meeting and the ladies saw you. We would like to meet you. Would you come in?"

I tell her I don't have long because I need to return to the house where I am staying. But I say a quick "hello" to the ladies, and we exchange requests for prayers.

As I am leaving, the lady tells me her name is Gretchen and says, "I have the keys to the church."

"I am so glad you told me that," I exclaim. "I need to pray in the church."

"I can arrange that," she says.

She lets me in the beautiful church, Our Lady of the Holy Rosary. I say the customary Our Father and Hail Mary, then chant the simple tone of the *Salve Regina*. Gretchen gives me her phone number and says, "Father, if you need anything, please call."

I go home and talk to my hosts, Shawn and Jennifer, about saying Mass that evening in the Jesuit High School chapel, as we had pre-arranged.

Saying Mass daily is so important because the Mass said with devotion extends the accidental Glory of God in the world. "Accidental" means that He is glorified in and by creatures. Of course God is perfect, so nothing can add to his glory because he is the epitome of glory. Creatures are accidental, meaning that they are not essential to God. Any glory we give is "accidental" glory, which does not add to God's essential glory, but, in a mysterious way, His accidental glory can increase in creation. God does not need accidental glory, but desires it for our sake. It is good for creatures to glorify God this way. The Mass extends this type of glory in

His Kingdom on earth. This is why it is so important that I say Mass every day, and why I am so intent on finding a place to say Mass after our plans fall through with the chapel at the high school.

I invite Gretchen to Mass. As we are setting up for Mass, I notice the day is a feria, a day not dedicated to a particular saint, and I choose the votive mass for the Propagation of the Faith. In that Mass, I continue to beg the Blessed Virgin Mary to make many things happen. She does!

Gretchen arranges for me to meet with her friend, a bishop. I tell her that I like to meet bishops who have an interest in the propagation of the Faith and tell them about the Rosary Walks, so they will pray for me and give me their blessing.

The next day, I go walking in the French Quarter with Fr. Jambon, a priest who lived with me in St. Joseph for a few months, and Jim Hitt, an acolyte in his fifties. We pass a man in his twenties, standing outside a bar, smoking. He yells to get our attention.

"What are you doing?" he asks.

"We came to the French Quarter to pray the Rosary and to talk to people of good heart."

"Well, I am Doubting Thomas. I am a military security guard. I called myself atheist, but now I am agnostic. I have been searching."

As he puffs on his cigarette, his friends attempt to distract him from us. Then, a biker revs his engine so loudly, we cannot continue the conversation until he drives away. But then comes a fifteen-minute discussion about God, religion and prayer.

"What is the story behind Mary?" he asks. "Why should I pay attention to her?"

He is asking that question to three men who are truly devoted to the Mother of God. We explain, with enthusiasm, how God loves His mother, and so we do well to love His mother too.

As we take our leave, we begin to pray the Rosary again. The man follows us and asks, "Could I have one of those beads?"

Of course, I smile and say, "What color do you like?"

I give him a pamphlet on how to pray the Rosary and teach him how to pray it. I also give him a Miraculous Medal and tell him that Mary draws many people to her son. There are many stories of people who once doubted God, but were challenged by their friends to wear the Miraculous Medal and ask the Mother of God for guidance, and they became totally devoted to Jesus.

"Why do you wear that chain around your ankle?" he asked me.

"We are all slaves either to the devils or to Mary. I chose to be a slave to Mary and give her everything I have. She keeps it for me and presents all my actions to her son Jesus." I smile and continue on my way.

Minutes later, we walk by a karaoke bar, and two men stop us. Max is in charge of the microphone and Joseph is a bouncer.

"We saw you earlier and wanted to talk, but we were busy," Max says. "What are those beads you are carrying?"

I explain how we contemplate the mysteries of Jesus and Mary while we walk around the French Quarter. After a brief explanation of the Rosary, they ask, "May we have one?" I give them each a blessed Rosary and pamphlet, "How to Pray the Rosary."

Just a few minutes later, we pass by a restaurant which has a hostess table out on the sidewalk. The hostess, two waiters and a bartender stop us and asks us what we are doing. We tell them about our happiness in serving God and how we want to share that happiness with everyone we meet. We explain that, by serving God, we will be happy in this life and in the next. "There are many ways to approach God," I tell them, "but one particular way we do it is by praying these Rosaries to contemplate the mysteries of our Redeemer, Jesus." After a brief explanation, all four ask for a Rosary and the pamphlet on how to pray it.

"Do not let me keep you from work," I tell them after handing out the rosaries.

"Father, do not worry," the bartender says. "Thank you."

A woman in her late thirties had overheard our conversation and has been waiting to talk to us.

"I saw you earlier," she says. "What are you doing?"

"We are teaching people who stop us how to pray the Rosary. Would you like to pick out a Rosary?"

"Yes, and may I have another for my friend?"

"Of course."

We continue on our way.

With all its raucous revelry and single-minded pursuit of amusement, sometimes it's easy to forget that there is a history of holiness also in the city of New Orleans. Fr. Jambone, a Louisiana native, enjoys telling me all about it. There was St. Frances Xavier Cabrini, Blessed Frances Seelos and Venerable Henriette Delille. We talk about the saints for a while, then Fr. Jambone asks me, "Father, do you want to see the Mississippi River? It is above the French Quarter."

I jump at the chance. "This Kansas boy needs to see this unusual geography."

We walk "up" to the river. It was so unusual to see the river above the Cathedral Basilica of St. Louis. As we are gazing across the river, a man and woman and their 12-year-old son walk by. The father says, "Dear Fathers, may our son get a picture with you and have a Rosary?"

We agree to the photo and give the boy a Rosary.

"We think it is neat to see priests dressed in the traditional way making a presence out here," the man says. "Our son was asking questions about you. We saw you earlier, but you were busy, but we were able to stop you for a moment here. I wanted our son to have a relic to remember what he saw." We conclude our conversation and take our leave.

About half an hour later, an old man in his late sixties approaches us on the sidewalk saying, "I had a dream that I need to look more to Mary. I am a Catholic, but I have been confused about Mary lately. I grew up with a strong liking for her, but my Protestant friends have challenged me on my devotion. But over the last week I have been dreaming of renewing my devotion to her."

Jim explains how important it is to have a love of Mary, as God has a great love for her.

"I have over two dozen nuns praying for all the people whom I meet here on the streets," I say. "They have been praying intensely over the last week. Perhaps you are receiving the fruits of their prayers, by these dreams. If this is the case, I am convinced that Our Lady interceded for you to God to give you these dreams so you would feel encouraged to stop us."

"Father, may I have a Rosary?" he asks. After letting him pick one out and giving him the pamphlet, we pray a Hail Mary and depart.

We run into three men in their late twenties, perhaps members of a band.

"May we take your picture?" they ask.

I give them permission, and after the photos are taken, they ask for Rosaries. Later in the day, three guys in their late thirties speak with us, and two of them ask for Rosaries.

A road worker spots us from at least a block away, according to Jim, and never takes his eyes off us as we approach.

"Father, you feed the world because you have been fed," he says. We launch into a fifteen minute conversation. He is the crew leader of two other workers. He volunteers one of his men to make a Confession because he lives a sinful life.

I say, "God does not force people to repentance. It is a gift. If your friend chooses to remain in his sin and reject the grace of conversion, it would be a sacrilege to hear his confession. We must be going."

A beggar approaches me, asking for money.

"Money I do not have to give to you, but I have some food in my backpack."

"Could I have some chocolate milk?"

"Yes." We continue to walk to a store as he tells me his story. I buy the milk for him, but as I am leaving he asks, "May I have a Rosary?"

I say, "What color do you like?" You have heard the rest.

Some guys are leaving a shop and they approach me. One of them says, "I saw you earlier, and I wanted to talk to you. May I have a Rosary?" As he is picking out the Rosary, I explain to him how the nuns are praying for him. I teach him how to pray the "Hail Mary," and how to use the beads with the pamphlet, "How to Pray the Rosary."

The next day is hot and humid, so we offer it up for the love of God and neighbor. We also make frequent trips to get cold, bottled waters.

A man approaches me saying, "Father, what are you doing here?"

I tell him, "I walk around the French Quarter and pray the Rosary."

"Father, we need you here. What can I do to get you back?"

"Say thirty-three Rosaries and God will help you know what to do."

"Father, tell me more."

"My dream is to have city monks chant the divine office, celebrate the Holy Sacrifice of the Mass in the mornings, come out to pray the Rosary on the streets, speak to the inquirers along the way, return for Vespers, a meal with table reading, recreation with the monks and lay men, Compline and monastic silence."

After he hears this he begins speaking to those around him: "This priest wants to do something that has not been done for a long time. He wants to start a new order." He turns to me, "Father, I want to keep in touch."

I assure him of that. He continues, "Father, I am forty-two, and my passion is music. Many of my friends have died in their late thirties, done in by a dangerous lifestyle. Would you have music in your new order?"

I respond, "Sacred Music!"

He says, "Father, if you would have said no, I would have walked away instantly."

"We must go, but can you promise me to pray some Rosaries?"

He nods, and we take our leave. -

A lady, who runs a small pamphlet and program stand sees us and asks, "Could you help me to receive my First Communion? My parents baptized me, but I never continued my studies to receive First Communion."

We have a long talk. I come to realize she is very intelligent and is seeking truth.

"Have you ever been enrolled in the Brown Scapular and the Miraculous Medal?" I ask.

"No, but I would like to."

After saying the prayers of enrollment, we ask her if she would like us to return with two important books, *True Devotion to Mary*, and *The Secret of the Rosary*, both by St. Louis de Montfort. She says, "Yes." We take our leave.

A few days later, we see her and give her the books. She says she is interested in taking classes to receive the Sacraments. She tells us about a lady who drives a Mercedes and wears an icon of the Divine Mercy around her neck.

"We have met her before," I say. "She came up to us and asked us about spreading the message of Jesus. She asked for a Rosary and I gave her one."

We take our leave and make a mental note to rendezvous with the woman who wears the Divine Mercy icon. A couple hours later, we see her!

"I cannot remember if you gave us your name, so I apologize," I tell her. "The lady at the pamphlet stand told us about you. I have something special I want to give you."

I take out a special packet containing the Rosary, brown scapular, the Miraculous Medal, the Litany of Loreto, the Morning Offering for the Brown Scapular, and two pamphlets for the total consecration to the Blessed Virgin Mary with a Brown Scapular. She is so excited she exclaims, "Father, could I have another one for my friend?"

"Certainly! The sacramentals are already blessed." We say our goodbyes and take our leave.

The French Quarter of New Orleans is home to many artists and musicians who perform on the sidewalk to make a living. Everyday, I pass a group of boys and young men tapping and clapping very loudly hoping the spectators will place money in their boxes. As I pass, I greet them with the customary smile and wave. On my fourth and last day in the French Quarter, as I pass one of the groups, a teenage tap dancer stops me and asks, "Can I have some of those beads?"

"Only if you can tell me what these beads are called. I'll teach you. Do you have a few minutes for me to explain the Rosary?"

"Yes, sir."

I explain how some Rosaries are made from rose buds, and that is why we call it a Rosary. I explain the "Hail Mary," how the angel spoke to the Blessed Virgin Mary. I show him how to hold the Rosary.

Then, I give him a couple of test questions. "Now what

are these beads called?"

"Rosary."

"Great, now who is Mary?"

"She is the Mother of Jesus."

I give him the Rosary he picked out, and as we take our leave, I look back at him, smile and wave.

"Thanks," he says.

A couple of hours later, Jim tells me, "Father, you did not notice, but after about a half a minute, I looked back at the boy, and he called after us, 'Thanks for the Rosary, Father.' Then about an hour or so after we met that boy, he must have been off work because he was riding a bike with his friend. I know you did not notice, but he saw us and said, again, 'Thanks for the Rosary, Father.'"

I enjoy some donuts in the French Quarter of New Orleans, compliments of some friends. We walk around the city and find our way to the Basilica of St. Louis to pray. When we walk out, I stand by the gate and gaze at the beauty of the basilica. An old man comes up to me and asks, "Are you Mennonite?"

"No, I am a Catholic Priest."

"It is great to see priests out in the public wearing their cassocks."

After a short conversation, I walk about fifty feet and a couple of young men in their early twenties come up to me.

"I like what you are wearing. What is it?"

"Oh, this is a cassock. The hat I am wearing is a saturno, like the planet."

They both laugh, and one of them says, "I really think it is neat. Could you tell me more?"

I tell him about the Rosary and the priesthood.

Standing in front of a store, a man in his mid-thirties

strikes up a conversation. He wants to know what the Catholic Church offers that other churches don't.

"There are many things, but I think the most important is the Most Holy Sacrifice of the Altar. We are given the Bread from heaven, the very Flesh and Blood, the Divinity of God. We share in the nature of God when we receive Holy Communion in a worthy state. Sinners turn to created things like drugs to numb their pain, but Catholics understand the importance of turning to the Creator to heal our sinfulness. Sin is in our blood, but God gives us His Blood to transform us into saints."

The man listens and responds.

"Father, I am a sinner. I am not drunk now, but I am going to drink ten beers before the night is over. I divorced my wife and left my kids, and I think I was born gay. I hate my life, and I know I need to change it, but I just do not want to right now."

I encourage him by telling him that the life promised to those who love and follow God is many times happier in this life and in the next. Then his friend, who is apparently shopping for a gift, comes out, sees me and says to me with a frown, "How do I know that you are not an imposter? Do you have a *celebret*?"

My inquisitor pronounces this word in Latin well. I was put on guard immediately, thinking, "Not very many people know what this word means and certainly fewer know how to pronounce it in Latin."

A *"celebret"* is Latin for "he may celebrate"—to celebrate the Mass. A priest requires permission from the bishop to exercise certain priestly ministries. A *"celebret"* is a card signed by a bishop, vicar general or chancellor who has jurisdiction in that area. It is like a badge that a police officer carries. I carry mine in my wallet.

"You have a right to ask that question, and I am thankful to provide you with evidence that I am a priest," I tell the man.

I open my wallet and let him read my "badge."

Meanwhile, the man I first spoke with rebukes his friend saying, "This is a man of God, and you are embarrassing him with your questions."

I interrupt. "He has a right to ask."

A number of spectators have come by. One of them asks me, "What do you think of Pope Francis?"

"He has written that we priests need to get out where the people are and stop being bureaucrats behind a desk."

Before I can continue the cynical man has moved to the fringe of the throng of people and exclaims, "If Pope Francis saw Father Carney and his disciple, he would kneel down to the ground and kiss their feet!"

I do not know what to think at this point. This man has made a complete conversion. As we wrap up our conversation to leave, the man says, "Thank you for coming here."

We walk to the corner of the French Quarter and a teenage boy walks up to me and says, "Hi Father."

I have a Miraculous Medal in my hand and stretch it out.

"Look," I say. "If you want it, I will give it to you."

"Yes."

"If you wear this and say three Hail Mary's every morning for a month and kiss the medal, something good is going to happen to you. It is not magic, but if you pray to God, He will give you a blessing."

I take out the pamphlet about how to say the Rosary, point to the "Hail Mary," and teach him how to pray it.

Jim and I need to walk around the block, where we have plans to meet up with a lady who is to drive us to an appointment. We walk quickly since we are running late.

We make it to our pick-up zone, and then we see the teenager again. He is reading the pamphlet we had given him. He looks at us with surprise. I thought he was going to say, "Wow! A miracle!" since I gave him the Miraculous Medal. Instead, he says, "Wow, you are fast!"

"Every moment that I can spend walking the streets is another chance to save a soul from the grips of Hell."

Photo by Gretchen Dyer
New Orleans

Photo by Gretchen Dyer
New Orleans

Photo by Gretchen Dyer
New Orleans

Photo by Gretchen Dyer
New Orleans

"For I know that we laughers have a gross cousinship with the most high, and it is this contrast and perpetual quarrel which feeds a spring of merriment in the soul of a sane man.

Hilaire Belloc
The Path to Rome

12

Gone Fishing

About a year after meeting those three band members on a downtown bench in St. Joseph, one of them comes out of his house and stops me on the sidewalk.

"I forgot your name," he says. "Is it Carney? Do you have time to talk?"

"Of course." I smile.

"My name is Brian. And by the way, what are you doing out here?"

"This is a Crucifix and our Lord Jesus is nailed to it. This Crucifix is a hook. Jesus said to His Apostles, 'You have been fishers. Now I want you to become fishers of men.' Every hook requires a line. This Rosary is my fishing line. I am fishing for men."

"I pray to God only," he says. We get into a discussion of his Protestant belief and our Catholic teaching. He asks me where I live. I take the CDs of the Nun's music out of my backpack. He invites me to sit on his porch and I show him the CDs.

"Yes, I remember you showing us those CDs when you allowed us each to pick out a sacred medal. I love Gregorian

147

Chant. I was in the Lutheran seminary in Covington, Kentucky, studying to become a minister. But there were times that I would take the day off and go to a church called the Immaculate Conception. There I could hear the beautiful chant of those in the choir. I also loved the beauty of the inside of that church."

I say, "Someone asked a Rabbi, 'How did Jesus pray?' The Rabbi explained, 'You Catholics have it. It is called Gregorian Chant. It has the eight modes that are from the ancient chants of our Jewish ancestors.' My dream is to get a beautiful church like the Immaculate Conception you visited in Covington, start a community of missionary monks and chant the Psalms in our sacred language, Latin."

"I love music and I would love to come to listen to that," Brian says. "Father, hold on a minute. May I go and get some books?"

I nod.

Brian returns with Greek, Hebrew and Latin Bibles. He noticed that I prayed the Psalms in Latin and tells me that he would like to learn Latin. As we are talking, a young woman comes up to visit with us. Brian introduces her as Jonni, a preacher, who helps the poor and bought a small church across the street.

"My roots are Catholic," she says, "and nobody can take that away. I always thought God wanted me to become a nun, but that never did happen."

I show her the CDs of the nuns and gave her my card.

"I am sure the nuns would love to receive you at their sung Mass." She says that she would love to go. I say my good-byes and continue on my journey.

When I return to the streets for my walk, a woman and her son pull up in a parking lot next to a busy street. She rolls down the window and starts a conversation. I tell her my story of walking the *Camino* in Spain. I speak of sleeping under the stars, being chased by a dog, running out of water in the Pyrenees Mountains. The teenage boy begins to perk up as I tell them both how I made about a thousand contacts by a picture or by a greeting. Since the response of a priest walking the Camino in the cassock and praying the Rosary was so good, I tell them, a nun and I thought about taking walks in the city here.

The woman, whose name is Monica, is happy to know what I am doing, gives me a small gift to buy some food, then departs.

A block away, I stand in the shadow of the Gothic church I mentioned before. Some people drive up, open the window and say, "Father, are you lost?"

"I am admiring that beautiful church. It is as if it cries to heaven saying, 'God, please send us Your blessing.'"

We chat for about ten minutes, and then they tell me they fell away from the Catholic Church years ago. I invite them to Midnight Mass in the Extraordinary Form. I am exuberant as I speak of the beauty of Gregorian Chant, which would be a part of that Mass.

"Father, we both like Latin!" they say.

I pull out a bulletin and write down the time and date of Midnight Mass.

"The pastor asked me to spread the word about the Midnight Mass. Do you think you will attend?"

"Yes!"

We talk a little more, then they leave because another motorist pulls up behind them.

I meet Jim, a man in his early sixties on a busy corner in West Wichita. He offers me a ride. He looks honest enough so I accept. We talk about airplanes and God. He said that he is afraid of Catholics because, at age seven, a Catholic classmate told him, since he was not Catholic, he was going to Hell. I try to comfort him with charity. As our conversation comes to an end, I invite him to Mass, likening the Most Holy Sacrifice of the Altar to a new Tree of Life, using references from John chapter six. We say our goodbyes and he lets me off to see my dad.

I take a group of young men to Fort Wayne, Indiana, to meet some religious who are Franciscans. We're welcome to sleep on the floor in the friary since the Father Prior and the Franciscan brothers are away in Mexico, except for a couple of the brothers who stayed to take care of the Friary. We eat meals donated to us and pray with the brothers. I say Mass for the Poor Clares nearby and the men learn how to serve the Mass.

One day, we decide to walk a couple of miles to a minor league baseball game. We become a spectacle--two friars in gray habits, myself in the black cassock and six young men walking and praying the Rosary. It is fun to watch the people react to the procession. We enter the ballpark, but there is no chance we are watching the game. We only get an occasional glimpse because baseball fans are coming up to us, one after another. I have immediate benefactors: "Father, can we get you some hotdogs?" "Father, how about I get you and the boys some popcorn?" "Father, let me buy you all something cold to drink."

And then this one: "Father, we own a meat locker. I know you are living with the Franciscans. Since you are guests, you rely on food donations. May we donate you some meat? Here is my card."

"Thank you for the offer. We will walk tomorrow."

The next day, those who volunteer to come with me leave for the meat locker after Mass. Along the four-mile walk, we pray the Rosary and the Psalms. Some passersby ask, "Hey Father, where are you going?"

"We are going to get some food."

People offer us drinks along the way and we have some conversations. After a couple of hours, we finally arrive at the meat locker.

"How may I help you?" the clerk asks.

"The owner promised us some meat," I say. "We met him at the game yesterday."

We are soon on our way back to the Friary with fifty frozen sausage links.

On the way, one of the young men in our group, a former Carmelite Monk, comments that this walk is such a fun and happy experience. The owner of the butcher shop had offered to drive us, knowing the Friary was four miles away. But we chose to walk. Think of the souls we might have touched that day by being visible on the streets.

When we finally arrive back at the friary, the two brothers and the rest of us fire up the grill and we enjoy some of the best food that I have ever had.

"Father, I am so used to eating peanut butter sandwiches that when I ate those sausage links, I got a bad stomachache," one of the brothers told me.

I myself got a stomachache, but not from the sausages. It was from laughing so much that day, being in the company of good friends and experiencing the joy of living your life strictly for the salvation of souls.

The idea of walking around town and making friends with the poor at the soup kitchen was inspired by my experience in Columbus, Ohio. It was there, in a former school building, that a priest started a soup kitchen. On the upper stories above the soup kitchen, he established a Catholic art museum of old altars, statues, candlesticks and other sacred objects. Museum patrons salvage church artifacts when Catholic churches are closed and donate them to the priests who wish to put them back into use. A community of sisters serve the poor in the soup kitchen and help with arranging for the spiritual needs of the impoverished as well.

While visiting one day, a sister approaches me with a request: "Father one of the homeless here just lost his sister to a homicide. He is so angry and he is telling us that he is going to kill the man. Could you talk to him?"

"Sure!"

I had been praying the *Breviarium Romanum* – the Psalms in Latin. After sister introduces me to the man, I look him in the face, smile and pray Psalm 26 in English. My book has the Latin on one side and the English on the other side. As I pray, I notice the living Word of God speaking to his heart. When I finish the Psalm, he takes the Breviary from me, looks at the text, closes the book and kisses it. I go to the adoration chapel and ask God to calm his heart so that he will not follow his desire to kill the man who killed his sister.

Back on the streets of Wichita, a man comes up to me one day and asks for some money. I say, as I usually do, "I do not give out money, but I am happy to buy food for you."

He is happy to hear that, so I ask what he wants.

"I want some Church's chicken."

"Sure, meet me at the public library in twenty minutes."

At the register, I tell the cashier, "I am buying some food for a beggar." I give her my order, a six-piece chicken box.

"Were do you go to church?" she asks.

I tell her I am visiting, but I sometimes attend Mass at Old St. Anthony's parish a few blocks away. She tells me she is from Salina and is looking for a place to worship. I wonder if meeting a priest in a cassock that day will be the motivation for her to return to church.

I find the beggar at the library. He smiles at me and says, "Father I used to go to the Catholic Mass many years ago. Now I no longer attend."

"My friend, today I have fed you with physical nourishment. As a priest, I speak for other priests. Return to the Catholic Church and ask to be fed the spiritual food that Jesus gives us. He once said, 'Labor not for the meat which perisheth, but for that which endureth unto life everlasting, which the son of man will give you.'"[1]

Another time, another beggar, this time near the Shirkmere Apartment Hotel in Wichita.

"Father, do you have some spare change?"

"Money I do not have to give, but food and clothing, I can get you."

"Yes, I would like to eat."

"Do you like Quiznos?"

He says he does, and we walk a few blocks there.

We arrive at the sandwich chain and place our orders. As we eat, the beggar offers his life story. He has done some bad things and has been in and out of jail.

"Father when I saw you, I thought you would not help me, but I wanted to ask anyway. When you smiled and offered me food, I was surprised. You made me very happy."

"Thanks for your kind sentiments," I say. "I am a priest, and I have a great desire to feed people with spiritual food. I hope you spread a positive word about me, because I have a great desire to be with the beggars of the world and feed them the food that does not perish."

After finishing his sandwich, he extends his hand. I shake his hand and he leaves. I continue to eat my sandwich and then turn my attention to God: "Dear Heavenly Father, this is what we need to be doing. Thank you for giving me such happiness by letting me help your people."

---

1   John 6:27, Douay–Rheims Bible

"They shall be the sons of Levi ... who shall carry the gold of love in their heart, the incense of prayer in their spirit, and the myrrh of mortification in their body."

St. Louis de Montfort

13

St. Joseph Comes Through

What surprises me about the Rosary Walk is how easy it is to talk to people. They are so hungry for God. A priest who constantly prays his Rosary around town for the conversion of sinners seems to be heard. I believe God will bless this endeavor if I am patient.

I am in the Hardee's parking lot when a man in his late sixties pulls in, opens his car door and says, "Father, I am so happy to see you. I have a question. Could we talk?"

"Certainly."

"Father, I have seen you around town and wanted to ask you something personal. I have stopped going to the Catholic Church." He tells me his reasons.

"Which parish is closest to where you live?"

He points at the Cathedral a few blocks north of us.

"Oh yes, Father will be very happy to help you with your situation. Just go there, and he will take care of you." I give the man some advice on how to work on his problems.

A young man and woman in their late twenties drive up next to me in a narrow street and roll down the window.

"Father, my friends love you," the woman says. "They have made many comments on Facebook and speak about the good you have done. You are like a hero to us."

"I just want to bring people closer to God."

She asks how to get in contact with me and whether she could schedule a time to talk and ask questions. I tell her where I live—during the week, in residence at St. James Parish in the city, and on weekends out in the country in the chaplain's quarters at the Priory of Ephesus, where I am the chaplain of the Benedictines of Mary, Queen of Apostles.

About three months later, the doorbell rings. It is the lady and a friend of hers.

"Father, I just wanted to see you, and tell you that you are awesome," she says. "My girlfriend also wanted to meet you."

I am honored to see them and speak briefly about God. I think to myself, "If these young adults are out to party, and they choose to take a break and speak to a priest at a rectory, this is something I think God could bless."

A few months later, I see her near the high school in South St. Joseph. She introduces me to her little girl. After a brief conversation, I ask the girl, "What is your favorite color?"

"Pink!"

"Oh, I have a pink Rosary," I say. "Do you want it?"

She smiles. "Yes."

When I am a block away from the end of my walk, I notice a group of high school kids a little distance from me. I smile and say "hello."

One of the girls comes up to me and asks, "Father, could you help me receive my First Communion?" She explains to me how she has been baptized, but stopped going to church

156

years ago as her family moved many times.

I tell her, "Yes." Our conversation continues for a little while and then we part ways.

When I get home, it occurs to me—I did not get her contact information. How will I ever find her? I decided immediately to go out and see where she is headed. I run out the door and walk the neighborhood, but I do not see the kids around any more. I immediately pray to St. Joseph: "Look at how bad I am! I cannot even get the contact information of a girl asking to come to the sacraments. St. Joseph, you have got to help me!"

The next day, I tell the nuns about my blunder and ask them to pray that I find the girl. I go to the St. Joseph altar in the church and beg St. Joseph to find her.

That afternoon I walk six or seven miles, asking St. Joseph in my Rosaries to find her. About a mile from home, I see two of the high school boys across the street. I really beg heaven that I will be able to talk to them. When I approach them, they ask, "What are you wearing?"

"This is a cassock. Do you know who Jesus is?"

They both respond, "Yes."

I pointed to the *corpus* of Jesus on my Crucifix. "Have you seen artistic representations of what Jesus wore? He wore a white robe. This cassock has the same form as the white robe. But we priests wear a black cassock because we mourn the death of our Lord Jesus. What are your names?"

The first responds, "Peter."

The other, "John."

"I do not want to keep you boys much longer, but do you have a moment to hear a story about Peter?" They nod.

"Peter was filled with God so much, that when cripples walked under his shadow, they were instantly healed. Peter, wouldn't that be neat if you were so holy, your shadow could heal ailments?"

They both smile. Then Peter recalls something. "Do you

remember Alice?" he asks me. "She wants to see you. She lives next to the protestant church, down the block from the park where she talked to you yesterday."

"Thanks boys," I exclaim. "You are an answer to prayer! I need to go and talk to her. It was a pleasure to meet you." We shake hands and depart.

I walk half a mile and then some friends pull up and offer me a ride. I ask them to drive to the house next to the Protestant church. As we drive, I tell them the story of meeting the girl who asked for instruction for First Communion, how I failed to get her contact, how I went to looking for her but could not find her, how I prayed to St. Joseph and asked the intercession of the Nuns and how I found the two boys who told me where she lived. When we drive up to the house, Alice is sitting on the front porch with her mom and step-dad, but then she gets up and goes inside.

"Oh, she probably does not want to talk to me now," I tell my friends.

I get out of the car and walk to the fence. "I am Father Carney," I tell her parents. "Your daughter met me in the park over there." I point down the block. "I am here to seek your permission to give her First Communion classes."

Alice walks out the door and greets me with a big "hello" and a smile. After a brief conversation, the parents give their consent for the instruction. When I get back to the van, I tell my friends, "Her parents gave permission for me to give First Communion instruction."

"Father, do you want to go get ice cream?"

"Of course!" I say, getting back into the van.

We have an ice cream party!

There's not always such a happy ending. One day in a residential area of St. Joseph, a gray car with tinted windows drives by the sidewalk, revving the engine. I bless the driver with the missionary Crucifix three times. The car turns around at the intersection, and the driver opens his window and says to me, "Hey do you want to smoke a bowl? I have some marijuana."

"No, I do not do that."

He asks me a second time and I decline again. He closes his window and screeches his wheels as he drives away. I pray the Miraculous Medal prayer: "Oh Mary, conceived without sin, pray for us who have recourse to thee." This devotion helps me when I meet with trouble. The rays coming out of Mary's hands on this image are either bright, dim or dark. Once asked why this is so, the Blessed Virgin Mary revealed that the dark rays signify rejected graces. So when people reject grace, I ask the Blessed Virgin Mary if I can receive the rejected grace. In charity, my intention is that if any of these people ever encounter me again, the grace that I receive from their rejection of grace, is stored by the Blessed Virgin Mary and is given them for their conversion.

One day, a young man, perhaps in his late teens, runs at me at full speed and hands me a note saying, "I cannot stay to chat."

As he departs in haste, I open the note to read, "Hail satan, 666, party with the beast, etc."

I look at the fast food restaurant that the young man entered, smile, drop the paper on the ground and jump up three times, landing on the paper with my heel. Some of the kids, along with the young man, came out of the restaurant, jumped up and down and yelled.

Seeing that these kids are not interested in any kind of meaningful dialog and just want to upset me, I turn my back on them, and continue my walk in peace, reciting the prayer, "Oh Mary conceived without sin, pray for us who have recourse to thee." I reflect upon the words of St. Louis de Montfort, "But the power of Mary over all the devils will especially shine forth in the latter times, when Satan will lay his snares against her heel: that is to say, her humble slaves and her poor children, whom she will raise up to make war against him. They shall be little and poor in the world's esteem, and abased before all like the heel, trodden underfoot and persecuted as the heel is by the other members of the body. But in return for this, they shall be rich in the grace of God, which Mary shall distribute to them abundantly. They shall be great and exalted before God in sanctity, superior to all other creatures by their lively zeal, and so well sustained with Gods' assistance that, with the humility of their heel, in union with Mary, they shall crush the head of the devil and cause Jesus Christ to triumph."[3]

I have seen that praying the Rosary with devotion and for specific intentions is fruitful, as St. Louis de Montfort preached. He also said that praying one decade of the Rosary with devotion is better than praying thousands of decades in haste and notes that the worst intention is to get the Rosary over with. He encourages the soul to have an intention for each Rosary and for each decade. I state the intention before each "Hail Mary," and repeat the mystery after each "...blessed is the fruit of thy womb, Jesus."

One day, I decide to pray for all Missouri Synod Lutherans in St. Joseph, Missouri, who have good hearts. An hour later, I am walking past a Perkin's restaurant when a young man hastily walks across the parking lot trying to catch my attention. "I do not see this outfit every day," he says. "Why are you wearing that?"

I smile. "I am wearing this so I can teach people about the happiness of union with God. This black garment is a cassock. Catholic priests wore it for centuries, but in the past few decades it has gone into disuse. Now young priests are beginning to wear it more. Our Lord Jesus wore a white robe of similar pattern to my cassock. The reason we wear black is to mourn the death of our Lord. But it is through His death that

3   St. Louis de Montfort, *True Devotion to Mary*, Tan, 1985.

we have life. The saints wear white robes and crowns of gold."

He responded, "Yes, we rejoice because we are called to rise with Him. I really appreciate what you are doing. I never see anyone wearing that and carrying a cross. I think we need to go back to our Judeo-Christian roots. Could I buy you dinner?"

I smile and accept the offer. "What is your name?"

"Jeffrey."

"I am Fr. Lawrence Carney. I would like to hear more about you. Could you tell me about yourself?"

He was happy to share his story and covered his family upbringing and his work life. "I grew up Lutheran. I like the Lutheran church, but I am searching out other churches, not so much to join them, but to see what they have to say. I think we are heading the wrong way as a nation. We need to get back to our Judeo-Christian roots and not have all the nonsense we have in churches today."

He explains that he had taken upper-level classes for a semester or two at a Protestant seminary, but he did not continue.

"Would you like me to speak about your desire to go back to Judeo-Christian understanding of our faith?" I ask him.

"Yes."

I begin to explain the Old Covenant foreshadowing of the New Covenant. "The Old Covenant offered sacrifice and holocaust to God in the Temple. The priesthood of Levi was separate from the sacrificial offerings, consisting of cattle, sheep and birds as bloody sacrifice and grain as un-bloody sacrifice. If the whole offering was burned, it was called a holocaust and considered most perfect. But if the offering was separated and only part of the victim was burned, it was called a sacrifice and was less perfect. In the New Covenant, the priest and the victim are one. Jesus is both the priest and the victim. He offers Himself to the Father, just as a priest in the

Old Covenant offered the holocaust or sacrifice to God. But Jesus offers Himself to the Father; whereas, the priest of the Old Covenant offers not himself, but another victim." I take my Crucifix and turn it horizontally, "See this. The altar is the cross and Jesus is the sacrifice. Sin is in our blood. God has revealed to us over salvation history how to make atonement for our sins, both individually and as a people or a nation. His revelation about making atonement has become more explicit over time. First, He required Abraham to offer his first born son. In the time of slavery in Egypt, God required the first born lamb to be killed and blood sprinkled on the door posts so the angel of death would pass over the family. When the Hebrews sprinkled the blood, they got the top of the door post, the bottom, the right side and left side. If you take those four spots and draw two lines, you form the Cross. Since sin is in our blood, God required the life of a spotless lamb without blemish, the first born to give its blood, its very life to save the life of the chosen people."

Jeffrey listens intently.

I continue. "On the day of atonement, once a year, the High Priest would go into the Holy of Holies to beg God to forgive his sins and the sins of the nation. The High Priest would wear a garment similar to my cassock." I pick up the hem of my cassock. "They would put little bells on the bottom, here. The assistant priests would tie a rope around his ankle. The High Priest would enter the Holy of Holies where no one else could see him. Before he did that he put his hands on the offering, the scapegoat like this." I showed him both of my hands parallel to the table, with thumbs interlocked. "This is what I do over the offering of bread, wine and water every day at the Holy Sacrifice of the Mass. The priest of the Old Covenant would do this to symbolize his sins and the sins of the nation going into the scapegoat. After it wandered it would fall off a cliff to its death and its blood would be shed. While this was happening, the High Priest would sprinkle blood on the altar. Every action and word had to be done within certain parameters. If he made a mistake, he would die instantly. The assistant priests knew that something had gone wrong when they stopped hearing the bells. Since no one but the High Priest could go into the Holy of Holies, they had to pull him out with the rope tied to his ankle. If he performed the sacrifice correctly and it was pleasing to God and the scapegoat shed its blood, a rug covering the threshold would miraculously change colors from crimson to white. Then the people knew their offering was accepted.

"At the Last Supper, the Anointed One, the Messiah, Jesus, offered bread, wine and water to the Father as a New Covenant for the forgiveness of sins. He told His apostles present at the Last Supper to, 'Do this in memory of me'." As I said that, Jeffrey joined me, "Do this in memory of me."

I continue, "You see Jeffrey, you know some of this stuff. The next day Jesus offered Himself to the Father on the cross as both priest and victim, shedding his Sacred Blood for the forgiveness of our sins."

I ask Jeffrey, "What is your favorite passage in the Bible?"

He tells me and then asks me mine.

"He who eats my flesh and drinks my blood will have everlasting life." I love John Chapter six. There are 'types' and fulfillments. Jesus said, 'Your ancestors ate manna in the desert, yet died, but the food that I will give you will give you eternal life.' John chapter six, verse sixty-six is very scary because His disciples followed Him all this way but had a change of heart. It says, 'And He said: Therefore did I say to you, that no man can come to Me, unless it be given him by My Father. After this many of His disciples went back; and walked no more with Him' (Jn. v.66). Some people claim Jesus was speaking symbolically, but whenever people did not understand Him, he would explain. Here Jesus says 'eat' not as a symbol, but literally. He does not run back to the disciples leaving and say something like, 'wait, what I meant to say was this eating is a symbol.' Rather He turns to the twelve saying, 'Will you also go away?' Peter responds, 'Lord, to whom shall we go? Thou hast the words of eternal life.' I find it interesting the number of the beast is six, six, six. The first apostasy, turning away from Jesus, randomly has been referenced by the number of the beast when people put numbers and verses to the Sacred Text."

Jeffrey seems to be taking in what I have to say about salvation history from a Judeo-Christian perspective.

"I will have to pray about all this, but it makes sense," he says.

"Now I have a question for you. What type of Protestant are you?"

He answers, "I am a Missouri-Synod Lutheran."

I smile and say, "I have something very interesting to tell you. Today I have done something that I never have done before. I prayed a decade of the Rosary for Missouri-Synod Lutherans, who have good hearts here in the city of St. Joseph. You are an answer to prayer, and it must mean that you have a good heart!" I give him my contact card.

"I am pleased that I got to meet someone with your conviction," he says.

"I need to go now, but if you yourself, or you and some of your friends would ever like to have more discussions like this at say, Dunkin Donuts, or some other place just contact me."

One day a lady in her seventies is working in her front yard as I walk by. She comes up and says something that I cannot understand. I ask her to repeat herself.

She says, "Thank you."

"What do you mean?" I ask. "Why are you thanking me?"

"Thank you for wearing that, carrying your cross and

praying your beads."

After we talk a little, she invites me to sit on her porch bench. She continues, "My mother was Catholic and I saved her beads. What do you call those?"

"This is a Rosary. Do you want to show me your mother's Rosary?"

"Wait, let me go get it." She returns with a beautiful Rosary -- very old with shiny crystal beads.

"Do you know how to pray the Rosary?"

"No."

"I am chaplain for some nuns. They make pamphlets called, 'How to Pray the Rosary.'

I give her one and as she looks at it she says, "Do you know how I can sign up to take instructions to become Catholic?"

I tell her the options.

About a year later, as I walk by her house, I wave and smile and she comes up to me and asks me if I would like to meet her grandchildren.

"Certainly."

As I am learning their names, one of the kids asks, "What is that thing you are holding?"

I lift my Rosary and point at it. "This?"

"Yes. What is that?"

"This is a Rosary. Do you want to hold it?"

"Yes." The other kids become curious and begin asking about the Rosary. I ask one of the grandchildren, "What is your favorite color?"

"Red." I get out my bag of Rosaries. "Is it all right if I give a Rosary to your grandchildren?" I ask the woman. She says it is.

After the kids pick out their Rosaries, I give them each the pamphlet, "How to Pray the Rosary?" Then I ask them to pray the "Hail Mary" with me.

It is cold and raining. I make my way from south St. Joseph to the downtown. Some young adults ask if I need a ride. I gladly accept. One of the girls says, "I felt sorry seeing you walk in the rain, so I asked for them to give you a ride. So we turned around to pick you up."

"You have a good heart. I am on my way to Cafè Pony Espresso downtown. Do you all know where it is?"

They say they do.

"When I was in Rome, I saw a lot of you walking around with that black hat and black robe," one of the young men says. "I really respect you. My name is Kay."

He gives me his custom printing business card.

When they drop me off, Kay says, "Come by and bless my office."

"Certainly."

About two or three months later, I visit. I get a chuckle when I see the slogan, "Fear kills dreams." Another one made me laugh too: "Everyone knows Kay."

The owner, a man in his mid-thirties, comes out the door and invites me inside.

"I am here if you still want me to bless your business," I tell him.

"Sure. What do I call you?"

"You can call me Fr. Carney."

"Fr. Carney, I see what you are doing, and I like it. Follow your dreams. I know some people make comments, 'What is that?' All they would have to do is look up an old movie on You Tube about a priest and they could get their answer. Some people just have small brains. I want to hear more about what you do. I have some kids who are part of a skating club. We do things for the community. I like to give service to the community. I see that is what you are doing."

I tell him my story—becoming a priest, finding my vocation within a vocation and my dreams. "I am praying that a bishop helps me to start a community of city monks who pray and walk the streets finding the lost sheep."

"That is great," he says. "Have you seen my slogan? 'Fear kills dream.' I grew up with great parents. My father disciplined us to be responsible and to work."

"I like entrepreneurs because they create something for the community," I tell him. "My family is full of entrepreneurs."

"All right," Kay says, "now bless my work."

I take out my stole, the *Rituale Romanum* and my Holy Water. I bless his business in Latin and translate for him, "Hear us, holy Lord, Father all powerful, eternal God: and send your holy Angels from heaven, to guard, protect, visit and to defend this house." I go around the office sprinkling Holy water, both inside and out.

He looks me in the eye and gives me a good handshake. I can tell that he is the real thing.

After I leave, I pray a decade of the Rosary for him.

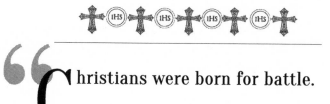

"Christians were born for battle.

Pope Leo XIII

14

Arming the Soul

Sometimes, this life I have chosen is hard, but I am reminded that I am not alone by something I wear upon my head.

Once, someone gave me a gift certificate to a Catholic goods store. At the time I was reading, *The Church Visible* by James-Charles Noonan Jr. He explains the apparel approved for the clergy. I was surprised to find out that the zucchetto, a black skull cap, is something that all clerics may wear except during Mass. So I saw a zucchetto for sale and tried it on. I was surprised that it fit, so I bought it.

Around the time I bought the zucchetto, two priests were attacked in Phoenix, Arizona. Fr. Walker was killed during the break-in. I attended his funeral in Kansas. My friend Helen gave me a cloth that was touched to the body of Fr. Walker before he was buried.

"Father, my friend asked the parents at the funeral if she could touch this cloth to the body of Fr. Walker. She gave me half of it and I want you to have it."

I took the relic, cut off a few small pieces and gave the rest to the nuns.

I took one of the Sacred Heart Badges a friend had given me and the cloth touched to the body of Fr. Walker and sewed them to the underside of the zucchetto. Before putting on my zucchetto, I kiss the Sacred Heart badge and say this prayer: "Sacred Heart of Jesus make my heart more like unto Thine. Fr. Walker protect me as I walk these streets." One of the promises of the Sacred Heart, "I will give to priests the power to touch the most hardened hearts," helps me to walk with hope in our troubled world.

I don't like to complain because I have been so richly blessed, but I have been advised by a good Bishop that it is important to talk about the struggles we face when we work for God.

All Christians have crosses to bear, but there are some unique ones for a walking priest. I have heard my share of gossip and negative comments about how I am going about my work to reach lost souls. What is most difficult is to hear these comments from fellow priests. Being constant in my resolve to continue with my mission is so important. I have great faith that walking priests are necessary in these times. Since the advent of cars, is so easy to go from one place to another and never meet anyone. But walking makes it easy for a priest to do what priests are ordained to do: teach, sanctify and bring people to God's holy altars. I understand why my work can seem impractical. Since priests are so busy doing important things and their time is so limited, why waste time walking?

The answer, for me, is easy. When a priest is walking and praying, he is doing what Jesus did. This is a sermon in itself. His presence on the streets shows that we need to slow down and do important things, make it a priority to pray and try to lead people back to God. I take comfort in knowing that my ministry mirrors that of Jesus, who also had both his critics and supporters. I am grateful, in times when discouragement might threaten to cause me to give up, that I do have those who encourage me to keep going, including those in the hierarchy of the Church. Such encouragement makes it possible for me to continue my ministry on days when my work can seem fruitless.

At times, it seems my ministry yields only broken promises. About nine times out of ten, when I exchange contact information with people who express their desire to meet again for follow-up discussions, they end up not returning my phone calls or emails. This hurts and shows my deep seated pride. What I have come to realize, however, is that people are going through a very difficult spiritual battle internally, and I am too. Temptations are strongest when one is making attempts to convert, revert or commit to God. It is so sad to see how God extends his hand, offering invaluable gifts, and people do not open their hands to receive His help. I have seen so many instances of people hurting because they want to have God in their lives, but they are reluctant to take that first "leap of faith" to come to Him.

Persistence is the answer. When people see me, day after day, week after week, month after month, and year after year, they can witness the stability of the mission. They can see by my actions that I mean to be steadfast through the struggles. We have to be like eagles and rise above. This is when God is prepared to give us the victory.

In the lives of the saints we come to understand how they overcame their predominate faults and how God used the virtues that came from this struggle to extend the reign of Christ the King. St. Augustine overcame impurity with chastity; St. Francis de Sales conquered anger with gentleness; and St. Ignatius of Loyola replaced his desire for romance with chivalry for the Kingdom.

After discerning that I was being called out into the streets to pray the Rosary, and after seeing the immediate fruits after only two months, it has been quite difficult to wait for this apostolate to become an authentic ministry of the Catholic Church. It has been almost three years since I have started this specific way of propagating the Faith. Along the way, the Church has given approval and encouragement, but in small ways, compared to what I would like.

A wise man told me that when something is of God it takes a long time for it to come to fruition. God has reasons for this. First, if the struggle is long, we appreciate it all the more. Second, a long struggle prevents us from losing God's grace. And third, practicing patience in the midst of struggle helps to purify us. So when people ask how the progress is going I say, "It is like watching an oak tree grow." I am confident, no matter how slow the growth is, God is behind it, and that is all I need to know.

Without the knowledge that God has called me to minister to His people in this way, I would not have the strength to go on. As I discerned my calling, I had to decide to leave home, possibly for good. It was hard to leave my family, my friends and the area a grew up with such happiness. I love my hometown. Growing up in Wichita was such a blessing. I developed so many relationships and these people encouraged me to do great things.

I still miss home. I struggle with going into new places all over the world. It was very hard for me to leave what I loved, but this is precisely the test that God gave me. Once I finally decided to do what I think God wanted me to do, I eventually was filled with such happiness.

My joy is knowing that I was born into this world in Wichita, but that I am a pilgrim, like all of us, and my happiness will only be found where God wants to place me. The Blessed Virgin Mary has desired me to fight in her military for the salvation of my own soul for the souls of all those whom I meet. The struggle is still there, but as each day goes by, I see how Providence makes it clear this is my vocation, to go out in search of souls in the streets and to eat with the sinners.

One day I am walking in Milan during a layover on a trip to Rome. A young Italian man asks me to have coffee with him. "I need to talk," he says.

I listen to his personal problems over a cup of coffee and then I encourage the former altar boy to pray and seek abandonment to Divine Providence. "Did you know that receiving the Body of Jesus Christ is the best way to overcome your problems? To receive the Body of Jesus worthily is a pledge against mortal sin. It will strengthen your resolve."

I decide to visit a number of churches while I am in Milan and make a mini-pilgrimage. I approach a church and find the gates to the courtyard locked. I walk around the corner and find another gate locked. As I look into the courtyard, I see a nun. She is an older sister in a beautiful black habit. When she sees me, she perks up. I do not know how to speak Italian, but I try to say a few things in Latin and just move my hands a lot. I tell her that I am a chaplain for some nuns in the United States of America and that I am making a pilgrimage to pray in the churches of Milan. She smiles, unlocks the gate and shows me to the parlor where she gives me a prayer card. I discover I am in the presence of the Visitation Nuns who were started by St. Francis de Sales in the seventeenth century. I explain to her as best I can my love for this order, how I used to serve Mass for a Visitation convent while a seminarian in Emmitsburg, Maryland. She then shows me to the grill where people visit with the nuns. I meet an elderly nun, who I think was the Superior. We speak briefly and I give them each a Rosary asking them to pray for my intentions. I take my leave, praying a decade of the Rosary for their intentions and thanking God that I found another convent of nuns who are willing to pray for me.

Back in the United States, I am walking down a hill in Independence, Missouri, toward three teenage boys. I am passing by a statue of Mary with her hands extended as on the Miraculous Medal, so I pray my Rosary, hoping to get a chance to speak with the boys. As they approach, I smile and wave at them. As we pass by each other, one of them asks something. I turn around and ask, "What did you say?"

"Are you an exorcist?"

"No I am not an exorcist, but I have friends who are exorcists."

Then follows a conversation about the practice of driving out the demonic and the various levels of demonic influence: oppression, obsession and possession.

"What are you holding?" one of them asks.

"This is a Rosary. It is a spiritual weapon against the enemies of our soul; namely, the world, the flesh and the devil."

"May I have one?"

I ask them each their favorite color and they all pick a Rosary from my Zip-loc bag.

I tell them the nature of sacramentals and disposal of them in case they get damaged. Then I gave them a pamphlet, "How to Pray the Rosary."

"I am visiting here from out of town, but the priest at St. Mary's has let me come to his parish. If you want to know more about the Rosary, talk with him. Do you know where St. Mary's is?"

They nod.

I am invited by Fr. Matt Bartulica to say Mass and do the Rosary Walks at St. Mary's and St. Cyril's. After the noon Mass, I begin a five mile walk to meet up with a priest. A parishioner picks me up and drives me about three miles then drops me off. I begin to pray and walk. After only half a decade of the Rosary, a van stops at the curb. The window rolls down. To my surprise I see two young sisters in brown habits and black veils. The driver says with a foreign accent, "Good Father, would you like a ride with us?"

I can never turn down a ride from women who have consecrated themselves to Jesus, their spouse, so I respond, "Sure. I am going downtown."

I absolutely love sisters and nuns so our conversation is very pleasing to me. The sisters tell me about their apostolate to the poor. One of them gives me their card, "Poor of Jesus Christ."

"Father, you are doing the work of God, praying and meeting people in the streets."

"Thank you for choosing to consecrate yourselves to Jesus your spouse," I tell them.

After they let me off, I find the priest at a coffee shop. We hop on a bus to get back to the parish, but soon we have to get off because a power line has fallen in the street. After walking a while, I realize that we are running late. Fr. Bartulica had asked me to say the Stations of the Cross at 6:00 PM. Not being from the area, I miscalculated the distance when we got off the bus. I leave the other priest on his own and begin jogging. After a few miles, I think, "I am still going to be late." I begin praying that God will get me a ride. Finally some young adults in their early twenties stop in and ask, "Do you need a ride?"

"Yes," I huff, out of breath. "You are an answer to my prayers."

I get in the vehicle and introduce myself to the three young adults. "Where are you headed, Father?"

I tell them, "I am going to St. Mary's to lead the Stations of the Cross. I am already five minutes late. Could you put the pedal to the metal?"

We have a delightful conversation. I mostly listen because I am catching my breath. One of them admits, "Father, I used to go to church at St. Mary's but I stopped going."

"My child, take this as sign from God to come back

home. We are your spiritual fathers and we want to help you receive the Body of Christ who will give you strength in the tough spiritual battle each soul has to wage on this side of eternity. I would talk more, but if I do not get into that church, they will start leaving for lack of a priest. Please do consider coming to eat with us after the Stations of the Cross."

I am in Covington, Kentucky, visiting two priests. While walking on the Ohio River levee and praying the Rosary, I notice two girls in the distance. I immediately pray for them. As they pass by, I smile, tip my hat and wave. In a few minutes, they both come running back, hollering to get my attention.

"I have seen you somewhere before," says 14-year-old Kayla. She is with her seven-year-old cousin.

"Kayla, I have never seen you before," I say. "This is the first time in my life that I have come to Covington, Kentucky."

I see charity in her face. I feel she is hungry for God.

"My friend just died in a car accident," she says.

"Let's pray," I say.

We pray the "Our Father," the "Hail Mary," and the "Glory Be."

I talk to Kayla and her cousin about heaven. I encourage them to become saints. A number of kids come up to join us on the levee. They listen briefly. The kids are playing some ball games down below so they bring their soccer ball. One of the boys says, "Kick it!"

I take the ball in my hands and drop kick it. The ball soars toward their ball courts. All the kids yell, "Wow!"

After they leave, I turn back to Kayla, "I want to ask you a big favor, but please do not do it if it is too much. Could you pray a Rosary for me every day for one month?"

Kayla smiles and says, "Sure."

I give her a blessing and we go our separate ways.

"My child, take this as sign from God to come back home. We are your spiritual fathers and we want to help you receive the Body of Christ, who will give you strength in the tough spiritual battle each soul has to wage on this side of eternity."

Photo by Jeanne Meyer

It is no use walking anywhere to preach, unless our walking is our preaching.

St. Francis Assisi

15

'Keep it Real'

On my first day in Phoenix, Arizona, I walk eight miles round trip from St. Catherine of Siena parish, where I am staying, to the downtown. As I pray my breviary and Rosary, I constantly have to fight back tears because of all the opportunity to do good amidst the 1.5 million souls who dwell in Phoenix. I think, "Jesus trained his Apostles, teaching them to become fishers of men. Jesus led them around the countryside, into the cities and along the lakes. Sometimes they were without a place to lay their heads. They were thirsty and often hungry. They were treated with scorn, but also with love. They drove out the devil and listened to Jesus predict the triumph of His kingdom by the sign of the cross." I beg God for the conversion of this city and ask Him to do everything He can through me to bring these people to His kingdom. Every city that I visit is the same. Some people see me and wave or honk the horn, and there are those who make fun.

I see a man walking in front of me for a while. He looks at the water as we cross the bridge. I pray fervently for him. A little later, he looks back at me and waits for me to catch up. He extends his hand.

"Hi, I am Vincent."

I shake his hand. "I am Fr. Carney."

Vincent tells me his story, and I tell him that I am praying for the city.

Vincent asks questions. "Father Carney, why do you wear black?" I tell him the usual answer: to mourn the death of Jesus and to show that I have died to my own will.

I continue, "I put myself into the hands of the bishop and promise obedience to him and his successors. I am here because I received the necessary permissions and blessings from the bishop, and I know that it is the will of God that I am here to see you." Vincent went on for a while telling me that he is not Catholic and confiding to me the mistakes he has made in life. He explains how he was supposed to die after a motorcycle accident, which caused his brain to hemorrhage. He tried to get up to pick up his motorcycle when his angel appeared to him and held him down.

I ask him to hold my Crucifix and Rosary as I teach him about the angels. "About a third of the angels fell from heaven and they were punished. The Blessed Virgin Mary was given the assignment to crush their head with her heal. The good angels and the bad angels are struggling to take your soul; the good will deliver you to the Kingdom of God and the bad will deliver you to the kingdom of hell. This Rosary is the second most powerful weapon against the devils because the Archangel Gabriel spoke to the Blessed Virgin Mary, using the very words we pray in the Rosary: 'Hail, full of the grace, the Lord is with thee.' These words are the foundation of the New Testament and put to flight the evil angels who tempt you to do the bad things you mentioned to me earlier. What is your favorite color?"

"Father, I am color blind."

As he continues to talk, I pull out the bag of Rosaries and a pamphlet.

He chooses a light blue Rosary. As I depart, Vincent says, "Father Carney, I hope to see you again."

As I continue on my way to downtown Phoenix, I think, "God, there is one soul out of 1.5 million. If I just meet a few thousand of them and make a good impression, the word will get around about a priest who walks around doing good."

Bishop Olmsted of Phoenix gave an interview on the Bishop's hour that I love. He was driving along and saw a beggar and rolled down his window to give him a bottle of water. The beggar said, "Are you Bishop Olmsted?"

The bishop said, "Yes."

Later he got a letter from a friend of the beggar, explaining how the beggar had died, but before he did, he told of Bishop Olmsted's kindness in giving him water. This is what the Church can do full time: acts of mercy that will draw people to the Church and Her holy altars.

I am waiting for some friends when two young men, one with dreadlocks and the other wearing a hat that makes him look like a rapper, approaches me. "So are you Amish?"

I had to chuckle inside as I smiled and went over to greet them.

I say, "No. I am a roaming Catholic."

I did not get their names, so we shall call them James and John.

"I saw you praying so I had to ask," James says. "So you do not get married? Why?"

"Jesus did not get married, and we voluntarily choose celibacy for the sake of the Kingdom of God." I launched off into my typical speech on spiritual warfare that I give to young men whom I encounter. "

"Fr. Carney, what if a man whom you met decided that he wanted to join you right now and walk with you? What would you say?"

I look him in the eye and smile, knowing that he has an interest himself. "I would say to that man, 'First, book an airline ticket to Rome for April 8th, because we need to meet together with a Cardinal to get advice about my Constitutions, a legal document that governs communities.' Secondly, I hope that man would ask this simple question: 'Fr. Carney, could you meet up with me and tell me exactly what your dream of a future community of men would consist of?'"

John smiles and says, "Yes, that is a great answer."

As they begin to say their goodbyes, I give them my priestly blessing, asking God to put in their heart a desire to follow after Jesus. As they are walking away, I catch their attention and say, "Keep it real."

They smile.

I have learned in life, that if we continue to put ourselves out in public in humility and with the fear of God, by our perseverance, we can do great things for God. I come from a family who works hard in life, but depends on God to bring our work to fulfillment. Imagine having encounters like this, say a million times in my life and in the lives of the men who join me. We would truly be fishers of men. Jesus told us to go out into the deep and make a great catch. Maybe men like these would become diocesan priests or join me someday, but they would be "bonus" priests that very likely would never have become priests if they hadn't met someone face to face, who is able to speak to them of the good and virtuous life they have been missing. Jesus went and found fishers and asked them to follow Him. These men were trained to mortify themselves by our Lord, and they respected Him, and eventually, with the assistance of the Holy Spirit, became martyrs for Jesus.

Some may say that an order like the one I wish to start will take away men from the diocesan priesthood. This is a challenging question. Our Blessed Lord Jesus found a group of rag tag fishers and nobodies, traveled on foot in the countryside and the towns with them, near the sea, in storm and calm, with hunger and thirst and even no place to lay heads. These nobodies became Apostles and we know their names and biographies. God takes the weak to make them strong. The new order will allow for His providence to find the weak, like myself, and make us great, by His power. He raises the weak and makes them powerful to confound the wisdom of the world. Men that otherwise would never come to a Catholic Church in their life, might very well be excited about coming and following me, walking through towns and cities in search of the lost sheep of the Shepherd. After seeing how such a community fasts and prays and travels, they might find they did not have the gifts from God to be a missionary. But this simple approach to propagating the faith might very well inspire them to join the Catholic Church, and discern a vocation as a diocesan priest. Diocesan priests have told me they consider the life that I live to be very difficult. I have received the gift from God to be a missionary priest, and I enjoy it intensely, but some priests are given different gifts and they help to feed the faithful as loyal pastors who baptize and bury, teach and govern a stable parish.

Photo by Jessica Trinidad Abril

Phoenix

183

Photos by
Jessica
Trinidad
Abril

Phoenix

Passing by a bus stop, I notice four people waiting. One asks, "What are those beads you are carrying?"

As I explain, I am interrupted by an onlooker. "Can I have some change?" he asks.

"No. But I can get you something to eat from the convenience store." I point across the parking lot.

"Can you give me some cheese puffs?"

I tell him that I can, but the first man interrupts: "Can I have a Rosary?"

I ask him what color he likes and he says, "blue."

As I am searching for a pamphlet about how to pray the Rosary, the other man gets mad. "You always interrupt me," he says.

Now I am chuckling.

"Father, do you have some food from your bag?" I begin to look and he continues, "And can I have a Rosary, too?" I nod, and pull out a Rosary for him. Then he says, "I want some cheese puffs."

I say, "Now what do you want? You keep changing your mind."

A couple of the others at the bus stop lightly scold him.

After I give him a Rosary and a pamphlet, I go to the convenience store. As I am searching for a bag of cheese puffs, an elderly lady asks, "What are you wearing?" I explain that it is a cassock.

"It is beautiful," she says. "I really like it."

I buy a large bag of cheese puffs take it to the man and say good bye.

All those people received a sermon from me, as though I was not preaching, just answering questions and giving them gifts. The image of the priesthood has gone through some trials in the last decades. But a priest in his full garb, authentically doing good for the ultimate intention of the salvation of souls, will one day renew reverence for the priesthood. A priest is anointed and called by God to bring Jesus into the world just as Jesus did when he walked along the countryside in the Holy Land. In the parish where I am staying here in Phoenix, the people have such reverence for priests, that they take my hand often and kiss it. The hands of a priest are sacramentals because they touch the Sacred Body of Jesus on the Holy Altar and they have been anointed with Chrism Oil at his ordination.

After Mass on Palm Sunday, a woman named Lynn asks me if she and her three children can accompany me on a Rosary Walk in the evening at South Mountain, after having dinner at her house. When we get to the mountain, I notice a hot dog stand. "That sure smells great!" I say.

The owner of the stand says, "Father, come on over, and we will get you a hot dog. What would you like on it?"

"Really?" I take out my wallet and say, "I want all the fixings!"

"Put away your wallet," he tells me.

"You can sit here," his wife says. "What is your story?"

I tell her the usual—that I am a missionary priest—and that Lynn had me over to eat today.

Lynn says, "They probably think that my cooking is bad."

"Oh no," I say, "I enjoyed the meal immensely! It is just that I am observing the great Lenten fast." I look at the woman who had served me the hot dog. "On Sunday's I can eat as much as I want, so being hungry only thirty minutes after eating Lynn's great cooking, I gladly accepted the offer of your generosity."

"Jesus fasted for forty days in the desert," I explain. "It is good to observe the fast which traditionally was one meal a day everyday during Lent. This allows us to imitate Jesus. If you take out the Sundays of the forty-six days between Ash Wednesday and Holy Saturday, you have forty days. I do not recommend anyone begin fasting this strictly all at once, but you should accustom your body to it over a few years. Start fasting one day a week after the Easter Season, then next

Lent you could try two days a week. Get a priest Confessor or spiritual director and ask for permission first." The Blessed Virgin Mary encouraged a spirit of sacrifice when she appeared to the three shepherd children in Fatima in 1917.

On Monday during Holy Week, I am walking back to St. Catherine of Siena, where I am staying during my visit to Phoenix, when a homeless man holding a medal crosses the street and asks, "Father, do you know what this medal means?"

"That is the Miraculous Medal!" I exclaim. "What is your name?"

"I am William."

I could not help but think, "This is going to be interesting!"

I told him, "William, you have been blessed with a very powerful sacred medal. If you pray the prayer, 'Oh Mary, conceived without sin, pray for us who have recourse to thee,' when you wake up every morning for a month, God will bless you. It is not magic, like we can control God, but the prayer is to ask for a blessing from Him."

During our conversation, the man tells me he is going to South Louisiana next week.

"What city and what dates?"

"New Orleans, March 30."

"You see?! Here is the first miracle. I am going to be in New Orleans the same time you are." "Meet me in front of the basilica in Jackson Square a week from Wednesday," he says.

I put it on my calendar and say good bye.

This encounter is a signal grace, the sort of fruit Our Lady promised to those who pray the Rosary. Such events are little sign posts indicating where God wants us to go. This is a prime example of Divine Providence at work. There are no coincidences, but only divine set-ups. Those who are invested in the Miraculous Medal, wear one and say the prayers receive these kind of signal graces too.

I continue my walk to St. Catherine's, and catch up to a

young man, about twenty years old. I notice he is wearing a Rosary.

"I like your Rosary," I say. "Where did you get it?"

He points to a store. "Over there."

"Have you ever learned to pray it or have it blessed?"

"No."

"Do you want to?"

"No."

"How are you doing today?"

"I am tired."

"Oh is that why you are walking slow?"

"Yes."

"Well, I do not want to bother you anymore," I say, "so I am going to walk on ahead."

He looks at me. "You are not a bother."

I see a bench up ahead. "Would you like to sit there and rest a little?"

"Yes. My phone is dead, and I have not been able to get a charger."

"Well my friend gave me two chargers, and I happen to have one in my bag. Would you like it?"

"For real?"

"Yes."

I take out the ready-to-use phone charger and give it to him.

"Oh no I cannot accept this. It is still in the package."

I insist, and he plugs his phone in, and it begins to charge.

"What is your name?"

"Jose. Father, why did you do that for me?"

I begin to explain spiritual warfare and the three enemies of the soul—the world, the flesh and the devil—against whom we fight very tough spiritual battles in our souls. Jose listens intently as I explain how the Holy Sacrifice of the Mass and the Rosary are the greatest spiritual weapons against evil. The Mass is like a nuclear bomb to the devil and the Rosary is like a canon. It is fun to aim these weapons at evil in the world, and the devil. These two weapons make us strong against temptation. At the end of our conversation I say, "Jose, it was an honor to speak with you today."

He looks at me and smiles. "Father, I will never forget meeting you."

He finally accepts a Miraculous Medal after I explain it to him, and I go on my way.

Every moment that I can spend walking the streets is another chance to save a soul from the grips of Hell. I have such purpose in life. I never get bored fighting against the devil. I have so many people praying for me, and that is why I receive so many signal graces and victories. The motto of the Martinian is *Ferens sacra in mundum,* "Bringing the sacred into the world." Jose is now wearing a sacred medal and he will remember how he got it forever!

On another day, walking in Phoenix, a middle-aged lady is waiting for me on the sidewalk.

"Are you a Father?"

"Yes."

"I saw you walk by once. Then I had to drop off my car to get it fixed and get another car. I saw you again and turned around and waited for you."

We begin a conversation about how she fell from holiness. I tell her, "Yes, the world is full of evil, and the devil is strong. But I know your Pentecostal background did not teach you about how much the devil hates the Holy Sacrifice of the Altar and the Rosary. When we receive Jesus, He is in us, and we are in Him. The devil cannot stop our spiritual growth when we become humble and receive Jesus in Communion and pray the Rosary. The Rosary is a battering ram against the devil. After explaining the Miraculous Medal and the Rosary and how to pray it, I give her four of each for her and her three daughters. Throughout our conversation, she cries such beautiful tears, as she reveals some dark things from her past and hears about how to fight evil. St. Louis de Montfort teaches that the Blessed Virgin Mary intercedes mightily for those who propagate the Rosary by example and teaching it to those who ask. Think of the huge victory that God and Mary had at bringing this soul who was a non-practicing Pentecostal to ask for Rosaries and how to pray them!

“Nothing can bring us into close contact with the beauty of Christ himself other than the world of beauty created by faith and light that shines out from the faces of the saints, through whom his own light becomes visible.

Pope Benedict XVI

16
Longing for Lost Traditions

My mom and dad both came from devout Catholic families. My grandparents had brothers who were priests and sisters in the religious life. They spoke very fondly of vocations. I would often see priests and religious at home or at my grandparents' homes. My father came from a large family, one of twelve. Grandpa Carney was the fire chief of Wichita (population 320,000) and worked as a janitor at Sacred Heart College. Grandpa Covelli built airplanes at Boeing. He worked at the "Black Hole," a department which built defense weapons during the Cold War. He never told us anything about that job because it was top secret. My parents and grandparents lived a very frugal life. Dad also taught me and my brother to save our own money to pay for college. Mom and Dad spent quality time with us, doing simple things: watching airplanes land at the airport, getting free tickets from the gas station for the local professional baseball game, driving around town, going to the park for a picnic, visiting the animals at the free municipal zoo. Mom and Dad learned how to stretch a dollar this way from their parents who lived during the Great Depression.

My parents, Larry Jr. and Kathie, were active in St. Joseph's parish, where we were enrolled in grade school. During the 1980's, three orders of teaching nuns collaborated to teach at this school. They included the Sisters of Charity of the Blessed Virgin Mary, the Precious Blood Sisters and the Dominicans of Great Bend. The Redemptorists ran the parish. I remember as many as five priests of that order living at the Rectory. Having all these religious in habits walking around the parish grounds had a profound effect on my vocation to the religious life. I was blessed to see the last vestiges of the visible church, the habit of at least four different orders located in one old city parish. They were quickly becoming extinct. St. John Paul II wrote about this phenomenon. Orders had begun to reject the strict observance of life according to the Constitutions of their founders, and so habits were disappearing.

Our parents would arrive at the parish about an hour before school started to drop us off at daily Mass. Attending Mass every day had a profound effect on my calling to the priesthood. Priests visiting my classroom and walking the grounds praying the Rosary made a big impression on me, too. Sr. Helen Marie, my second and fourth grade teacher taught from the Baltimore Catechism and a strict regimen of prayer in the classroom: the Angelus in the morning and before lunch and at other times a portion the Rosary and other devotional prayers. The sisters decorated the classrooms with religious art. Sr. Helen Marie took a liking to me and encouraged me to collect stamps. She let me study her stamp collection, encouraged my parents to buy a stamp collecting book and gave me some of her stamps. This was the beginning of my love for history, which has evolved into a passion for Catholic History.

I was born on
November 11, 1975,
in Wichita, Kansas,
the oldest of three
brothers.

Photos courtesy of
the Carney family
photo album
Wichita, Kansas

First Holy Communion, November 20, 1983, St. Joseph Church, Wichita, Kansas.

One of my friends who received his First Communion that day also became a priest.

Photos courtesy of the Carney family photo album
Wichita, Kansas

My grandfather, Nick Covelli, liked to take us fishing, but I did not like it because I did not catch enough fish. I have learned more patience now as I fish for men. The "fish" are biting more.

"Often the memories of my grade school years bring tears to my eyes. I thank God constantly for this experience, and I wish to devote my whole life to bringing back this Catholic culture for the next generations. My heart is on fire to bring this experience to others."

I firmly believe that we must educate the youth with truth, beauty and goodness, with all the Church has to offer, especially her lost traditions.

My mother stayed at home to raise us kids, keep the house and work on her hobby of sewing, which has now evolved to sewing vestments for priests. When I was a seminarian, I visited the archives of Mount St. Mary's Seminary and saw a Marian vestment from the eighteenth century.

"Do not touch that vestment," the caretaker said, "It will disintegrate. That was made by the mother of a priest who re-made her wedding dress into a Marian vestment for her son. That was the custom at the time."

I was inspired to ask Mom to do the same. She found her old wedding dress, washed it and made me one of the most beautiful chasubles I have ever seen.

Dad worked as a banker, eventually becoming the president of one bank and then another. Finally, he ended up owning his own bank.

Families are rarely perfect. Dad told us about the "black sheep" of the family as an example of how not to live. But my parents emphasized the good things our ancestors did. Grandpa Nicholas Covelli, a hundred percent Italian, told us we came from nobility in Calabria and Sicily. One of our ancestors discovered an element that is so rare, according to Grandpa, it is not even on the chart of elements. My dad's cousins founded Pizza Hut in Wichita, Kansas.

Another heritage from my family is a love of walking. Dad used to take me and my brothers, Anthony and Vincent, on walks to the local golf course and search the woods for golf balls. It was like an Easter Egg hunt. My little brother was not so wise in the beginning. When he would see a golf ball he would point it out, then one of us older brothers would outrun him to get it. He eventually learned not to call attention to the balls he spotted. Dad also had us walk a mile or so to downtown Wichita. He would take us through all the buildings. One building had a secret door. It was camouflaged to look like a mirror, but dad would say, "Can you find the door over there?" We were probably ten, eight and six at the time; so we would search for awhile, and he would finally show us. He showed us other fascinating things, like how money comes out of ATM's. He also liked to take us on all the second-level pedestrian bridges that crossed the streets and connected the buildings.

I guess I still love that sense of adventure. I know each day is going to bring something new in my journeys, and I will find something much more important than golf balls.

One day in St. Joseph, an elderly lady stops me on the corner.

"Father, I met you a few months ago when you were walking. Do you have a moment?"

"Yes, could you tell me your name again?"

"Mary."

The woman speaks about her life with Jesus, living as a Catholic. As I listen, I come to find out that she has stopped attending Mass regularly.

"Mary, it is important to receive the Body of Christ in the Most Holy Sacrament of the Altar," I tell her.

She agrees. I give her my blessing before we part.

A month later, I get a call from the parish secretary.

"Father, Michelle Kearney's family wants you to visit her. She is dying. They said that you brought her back to Church."

I get off the phone and walk eight miles to the hospital. Michelle asks for the Last Rites, Confession, Anointing of the Sick and the Apostolic Blessing. I encourage the family to speak with the local pastor to make the funeral arrangements.

A seminarian who visits Michelle regularly tells me that Michelle cannot stop talking about our brief encounters on the street.

She passes away soon after my visit. The priest assigned to the Mass asks me to preach a sermon. I encourage the people at her funeral to come back to receive the Sacred Body of Christ. Many of them have abandoned the Catholic faith. Some have never known it.

"I know it may be hard to come to church," I say. I pull out my Rosary. "This Rosary makes it very easy because we use these beads to repeat the words in the Bible about the mercy of God and our joy that He gave us a Redeemer."

Maybe some of them will try it. Maybe it will lead them back, and our pews will be full with those whom they were once missing.

This is why I walk the streets. For people like Michelle. For people like her loved ones who come to her funeral. That one act of love they show by coming to bid her farewell may someday multiply and bring them to their salvation, all because a priest in search of the lost spoke a word into their hearts. This is why I walk. And this is why I pray.

Photo by Jeanne Meyer

"We are given the bread from heaven, the very flesh and blood, the divinity of God. We share in the nature of God when we receive Holy Communion in a worthy state. Sinners turn to created things like drugs to numb their pain, but Catholics understand the importance of turning to the Creator to heal our sinfulness. Sin is in our blood, but God gives us his blood to transform us into saints."

Photo by Jessica Trinidad Abril

Bibliography/Sources/Suggested Reading

True Devotion to Mary, St. Louis de Montfort, Tan Books
The Glories of Mary, St. Alphonsus de Ligouri
Introduction to the Devout Life, St. Francis de Sales
The Cleaving of Christendom, Warren H Carroll
Audiutricem Populi, Encyclical, Pope Leo XIII
Rosarium Virginis Mariae, Apostolic Letter of Pope John Paul II
Mother Teresa: In My Own Words, Jose Luis Gonzalez-Balado
Into the Breach: An Apostolic Exhortation to Catholic Men, my Spiritual Sons in the Diocese of Phoenix, Most Rev. Thomas J. Olmsted
For Them Also, Most Rev. Charles Francis Buddy
Sulpitius Severus on the Life of St. Martin, Nicene and Post Nicene Fathers
Verbi Sponsa: Instruction on the Contemplative Life and on the Enclosure of Nuns
Sermon on the Dolors of Mary, St. Alphonsus de Ligouri,
Everything You Ever Wanted to Know About Heaven, but Never Dreamed of Asking, Peter Kreeft
The Secret Life of the Rosary, St Louis de Montfort
The Church Visible, James Charles Noonan Jr.
Mother Teresa: Her Essential Wisdom, Ed. Carol Kelly-Gangi

Rosary Meditations from Caritas Press

A MOTHER'S BOUQUET: ROSARY MEDITATIONS FOR MOMS

Straight from the heart of a mother, these rosary meditations for moms will uplift and sanctify your journey. Sherry Boas, author of the critically acclaimed Lily Trilogy, offers these prayers in hopes that moms will grow in holiness and come to more fully treasure the wondrous vocation of motherhood enfolded in the mysteries of Christ's life, death and resurrection. **By Sherry Boas** AVAILABLE IN FULL-COLOR GIFT EDITION AND IN SPANISH

A FATHER'S HEART: ROSARY MEDITATIONS FOR DADS

Discover the heart of true fatherhood as it relates to the life, death and resurrection of Christ. With pearls of wisdom and glimpses into the eternal and relentless love of God, Father Doug Lorig draws on his own experiences as a father and pastor to bring parents to a deeper understanding of their role in God's perfect plan of salvation. Grow in holiness within the wondrous vocation of fatherhood as you pray these rosary written especially for dads. **By Father Doug Lorig**

GENERATIONS OF LOVE: ROSARY MEDITATIONS FOR GRANDPARENTS

Get a glimpse into the heavenly realities of grandparenthood as you come to understand the beautiful and invaluable role you play as parents of parents. Through these insightful and uplifting meditations, Author Anne Belle-Oudry reminds us that, while grandchildren are undoubtedly among life's richest rewards, grandparents, too, are an inestimable blessing to their families as they strive to lead their loved ones closer to Christ through their prayers, example and unconditional love. **By Anne Belle-Oudry**

A CHILD'S TREASURE: ROSARY MEDITATIONS FOR CHILDREN

Grow to love the Lord more deeply through these meditations written by children for children. With insight into how Mother Mary loves Jesus, authors Derek Rebello, Elsa Schiavone and Michael Boas show us how to follow Him more closely in our everyday lives and discover that our faith is truly our greatest treasure. **By Derek Rebello, Elsa Schiavone and Michael Boas**

AMAZING LOVE: ROSARY MEDITATIONS FOR TEENS

Grow to understand the unsurpassed importance of your friendship with Jesus through these rosary meditations written by teens for teens. Authors Mari Seaberg, Adrian Inclan and Maria Boas show how the passion, death and resurrection of Christ sustain our lives today as we strive to do His will in the face of a multitude of decisions, illuminated by his amazing love. **By Adrian Inclan, Mari Seaberg and Maria Boas**

A SERVANT'S HEART: ROSARY MEDITATIONS FOR ALTAR SERVERS

Prepare your heart for true service with these Meditations written especially for altar servers. Reflect on the meaning of your calling as it relates to the mysteries of Christ's life, death and resurrection and as it applies to your own life in a world that is often at odds with the message of Christ's self-sacrificing love. **By Peter Troiano**

Visit CaritasPress.org

Other Titles From Caritas Press

 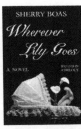 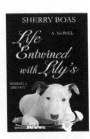

Until Lily
Wherever Lily Goes
Life Entwined with Lily's
The Things Lily Knew
Things Unknown to Lily
A Little Like Lily

 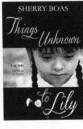 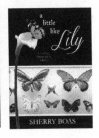

"...You will be entranced, you will experience the joys and sorrows of the characters, you will cry, and you will not be able to put Lily down."
– Dr. Jeff Mirus of CatholicCulture.org

The transforming power of love is at the heart of Sherry Boas' poignant series about the people whose lives are moved by a woman with Down syndrome. Lily's story is told with such brutal yet touching honesty, it will have you laughing one minute and reduced to tears the next.

Wing Tip

Dante De Luz's steel was forged in his youth, in the crucible of harsh losses and triumphant love. But that steel gets tested like never before as his mother's deathbed confession reveals something startling about his father and presents the young Catholic priest with the toughest challenge of his life, with stakes that couldn't get any higher.

"Sure to be a Catholic Classic"
"Magnificent read"
Robert Curtis, Catholic Sun

Visit CaritasPress.org

Children's Titles from Caritas Press

Miraculous Me

What thoughts crossed your mother's mind the first time she laid eyes on you? What dreams did your father hold in his heart? This delightful story by Ruth Pendergast Sissel is told from the perspective of a baby in the womb, listening to his parents' awe at seeing him on ultrasound for the first time.

Prolife Books!

Barnyard Bliss

The animals can't wait to share the news, Something exciting and beautiful has come to be! A new baby enters the world! All of creation rejoices as word of Mr. And Mrs. Hoot's owlet spreads throughout the farm.

With unbridled joy, their voices rise. All things old, become refreshed Welcome Babe! A joyous day! We pray your life be blessed!

Encyclopedia of Peg Saints

Discover all the fascinating facts that make the saints so lovable and inspirational. Get to know 36 saints in an engaging and easy to "absorb" format, centered around colorful hand-painted peg dolls collected and cherished by Catholic kids everywhere.

God's Easter Gifts

Bella and Pablo love Easter egg hunts. So many wonderful goodies just waiting to be found inside each egg! But the brother and sister are about to discover there's much more to Easter than candy and toys, as they embark on a very special Easter egg hunt that will reveal all of God's greatest gifts to us.

St. John Bosco & His Big Gray Dog

It is hard to believe that anyone would have ever wanted to hurt good Father John Bosco. He helped so many people. But there were times when his life was in danger. During those times, a very special guardian would appear to protect him. In this way, God saved the holy priest from harm so he could complete his mission and help children come to know God.

Visit CaritasPress.org